A Lived Life

Reflections on A Buddhist Life

By

The Venerable Deok Wun

First Edition

January 2016

Available from Amazon.com and other retail outlets

Available from createspace.com

Also Available on Kindle and as an audio book

ISBN-13 978-1522988694

ISBN-10 1522988696

Copyright 2015

No part of this book may copied or transcribed without the express, written permission of the author.

Table of Contents

Introduction	5
Forward	7
The Fundamental Fear	11
Atonement	27
Where is the mind? What is myself?.	45
Compassion	63
Understanding and Wisdom	70
Joy in Action	91
The Power of Commitments	100
The Eight Winds of Discontent	121
The Mind of No Anticipation	139
A Lived Life	151
Selected Bibliography	169

Introduction

This book is a transcript of a series of Dharma Talks delivered by the Venerable Deok Wun, Abbot and Guiding Teacher of the Grand Rapids Buddhist Temple and Zen Center. These talks were recorded and transcribed by the temple Sangha during the Fall Practice Period of 2014 (September thru December).

The theme for the series, a *"Lived Life"*, was chosen by the Venerable Deok Wun based on his study of the work of the Indian Mystic, Osho, the works of the Tibetan Yogin, Shabkar, The Way of the Bodhisattva by Shantideva, other teachers and masters, as well as his own experiences with the teachings of the Buddha. He developed this series of talks both as instruction and a way of personal reflection and discovery. He also stresses Master Dogen's admonishment that, "to study the Buddha Way is to study the self. To study the self is to forget the self". The overarching theme of these talks is that of engaging a *Lived Life*.

On behalf of the Grand Rapids Buddhist Temple and Zen Center, Grand Rapids, Michigan, we hope that you will find these teachings helpful as you explore how to live your life with love, happiness, compassion, kindness and joy.

In the Dharma,

The Grand Rapids Buddhist Temple and Zen Center.Grand Rapids, Michigan.

Forward by The Teacher

I am convinced that each of us wants to live our lives in such a way that we are free from the stresses and distractions that keep us from being authentically alive. By that I mean, we want a life that is flowing with love, compassion, kindness, joy, peace, and yes, even bliss. This is what the Buddhas have taught over the eons. As I continue to encounter people who come looking The Buddha Way as the vehicle for changing their lives, I am struck by how difficult it is for many of them to transform their intent to change their lives into the very change they desire.

I remember how difficult living an authentic life was for me. In my case, I was plagued by fears---many of them. As I continued to explore who I was, I wondered if there wasn't one, fundamental fear that was driving all my other fears. I never tried to name my fears. I allowed them to manifest over and over again as frustration and anger. There was little room for kindness or joy because I put so much energy into my frustrations and anger. Just when I had reached the point where my frustration and anger were taking over everything in my life, I realized that I had to choose to either align how I lived my life consistent with the Buddhas' teachings, or continue to live unauthentically. When I came to this crossroad I stumbled on the teachings of the Indian mystic, Osho. He identified that fundamental fear for me. It wasn't some convoluted fear nor was it an irrational or pathological fear. The fear he pointed out to me was so simple, so "right", that it eventually brought me all the way back to the heart of The Buddha Way. This fundamental fear, I discovered, is really the only fear that we all have. Yes, it shows up wearing many disguises, but once we take off the masks of all those fears we reveal only one fear: the fear of a lived life.

This was a life changing moment for me though many questions remained. What is this fear of a Lived Life, really? How was I to get to know it? How was it keeping me away from knowing myself? Or, was coming face-to-face with this fear the way into myself? As a Zen practitioner I knew that I had to come to know myself intimately. It would only be with this knowledge that I could, as Master Dogen says, "forget the self". After many years of exploring the answers to my questions about what is a Lived Life, I came to the realization that Osho was right: *what I feared most was a Lived Life.* I was terrified of making the changes necessary to live authentically, and I was blind as to the ways to move from where I was to a fully engaged life where I could live from a place of kindness, compassion, joy, and authenticity. Eventually I was able to make that transformation. It was not easy.

The series of Dharma Talks transcribed in this book are based on my personal experience with coming to the place of a *Lived Life.* It is my hope that these talks might prompt anyone who is so inclined, to face their own fear of a *Lived Life* and move to a life of joy. Not every teaching in this book will resonate with you. I recommend that you set aside all your judgments and opinions about what you read and pay attention to how what you read creates reactions in you. Perhaps in those reactions you can come to see this fear in yourself and use it as a way to deepen your life and life it more authentically.

Let me also invite you to contact me at anytime via email at deokwun@grzen.org.

The Fundamental Fear

Today we begin the Fall Practice Period. In the Buddhist Tradition there are typically two practice periods a year. Historically, each was aligned with the rainy seasons where it was difficult for the monks and nuns to travel. During these practice periods the monks and nuns would remain in their home temples for study, contemplation, and work. They increased their efforts in each of these areas and worked closely with their teachers. Each period lasted about 90 days. Between the practice periods the monks and nuns would travel and visit other teachers and monasteries. It was traditionally only something the monastics did. It was never a practice for lay people. Today, in the United States, we don't have monastic communities and we are trying to morph monastic practice opportunities into experiences for lay practitioners. We have families, go to work or school, are generally quite busy. We must guard against using these as excuses to avoid paying attention to our practice or intensifying it for just a little while. We don't ask that you try to emulate monastic practice, but we do ask that you take time occasionally to enhance your practice. So, today we begin a roughly 90 day period where we are asked to boost our level of commitment to be present and active here at the temple, in its activities, and to be more present in our daily lives.

Why should would take some time twice each year to deepen our commitment to our practice? The answer is simple: to strengthen the authenticity of our lives.

Again, historically, each practice period has a theme. Our theme for this Fall's Practice period is: *A Lived Life*. We will do our best to embed this theme in all that we do from now through the celebration of Buddha's Enlightenment in December.

Why this theme, "*A Lived Life*"? I have chosen this theme because most of us, and that includes me, are, or were, afraid to live our lives so that we are fully engaged in it and without fear of what our lives may hold. By the time we reach the end of this practice period you will know how to live a fully engaged life. You will come to see the potential that is within you to live happily and joyfully. We will spend the next several weeks laying the foundation for our *Lived Lives* and then we will build the scaffolding that will support it. Our first step in laying the foundation for a *Lived Life* is understanding that one thing that keeps us from this lived, joyful life. FEAR!

The Indian mystic, Osho, suggests that all of us share one, fundamental fear---the fear of a lived life. Whether you agree with him or not, I'm asking that for the sake of this practice period you consider that he might be right. In other words, let's all say, "yes" to this fear of a *Lived Life*.

Saying yes to our fears is not saying we accept them. Instead, we are wholeheartedly admitting that they are there and we aren't going to hide or run away from them. Zen teacher Ezra Bayda, of the San Diego Zen Center, puts it this way:

> *What does it actually mean to say yes to our fear? It means we're willing to open to it and embrace it as our path to freedom. Saying yes doesn't mean we like it---it simply means we're willing to feel what it really is.*

Let's all admit and accept that we all have a fear of a *Lived Life*. Why? To truly live an authentic, engaged, and joyful life we have to confront the expectations that have been set in front of us. Some of them have been placed there by others, like our parents or spouses. Many, perhaps too many, have been placed there by us! We may have to expose others to their own disappointments in us. We will have to acknowledge and let go of our disappointments in ourselves, and we have to take risks, real risks, risks that we are dying to take, but are terrified to take for a whole litany of reasons and excuses, none of which matter in the end. In short, to choose a lived life is to choose to be completely and utterly free. This takes courage and strength. But, if we admit that we have this fear of a lived life, can accept it, and choose the risk of freedom and authenticity, then what would our life be like? Think about it: what if every minute of your life was fearless? Can you imagine the freedom in that? If we truly are authentic and free, we can come to the point of being able to say without hesitation, "I am living".

If you are willing to take that risk, then you must, as a Buddhist, ask yourself: what is a *Lived Life*? As you consider this question I'd also like you to set aside every single idea, notion, or thought that has just arisen in your head as you heard the question. Approach the question with a clean slate: just let the question sit and see what arises as we explore the notion of a *Lived Life*.

One more thing I want to say as we begin. I am assuming that each of you is here because on some level you have decided that you want more from your life. That you have reached a point where you are asking yourself, "there must be more than this". Maybe this is a conscious thought for you and maybe it isn't, but I can assure you that somewhere inside of you this question is itching to be scratched. It's time to scratch it.

I want to share a story with you. It is called, "Watch Yourself"

> There was once a pair of acrobats. The teacher was a poor widower and the student was a young girl by the name of Meda. These acrobats performed each day on the streets in order to earn enough to eat.
>
> Their act consisted of the teacher balancing a tall bamboo pole on his head while the little girl climbed slowly to the top. Once to the top, she remained there while the teacher walked

along the ground.

Both performers had to maintain complete focus and balance in order to prevent any injury from occurring and to complete the performance. One day, the teacher said to the pupil:

'Listen Meda, I will watch you and you watch me, so that we can help each other maintain concentration and balance and prevent an accident. Then we'll surely earn enough to eat.'

But the girl was wise, she answered, 'Dear master, I think it would be better for each of us to watch ourself. To look after oneself means to look after both of us. That way I am sure we will avoid any accidents and earn enough to eat.'

What's the lesson here? How does this story inform our theme of *A Lived Life?*

Just like the girl and the teacher, if we are to live our lives fully, we must maintain focus and balance. First, we must focus on uncovering our fear of a *Lived Life* and all that entails. When the girl speaks of balance, she is saying that if we tip to one extreme of the other we will fall. Just like the girl and the teacher, we too can achieve a balanced, fear free life when we first take care of ourselves. This may sound selfish. It may seem contrary to what you think you know about what the Buddha teaches about the self, but remember that the Buddha said, "the only real failure in life is not to be true to the best one knows." The Buddha is telling us to start first with knowing ourselves and to do this we must come to experience the fear we have of living our lives.

A *Lived Life* is an authentic life. It is a life that begins with just us. Yes, the welfare of others will ultimately be our focus, but how can we be of any benefit to others if we are not first truthful and authentic with ourselves?

delight full of a panoramic vision of love? I'd wager just about every one of us wants this.

Reflection:

Consider each of the following statements. Take a few minutes between each one to be still and silent. Instead of just observing the thoughts that arise as many of us have been taught to do, this time look at each thought and ask, "why am I having this thought"?

1. Am I living my life the way I want to live it?

2. What would my life look like if I could chose it to be exactly how I want it to be?

3. What obstacles do I see to living my life fully?

4. How do I describe the fears I have about living my life?

5. Do I want to live with this fear or learn to set it aside?

Atonement

Shantideva said:

> *All you who would protect your minds*
>
> *Maintain your mindfulness and introspection*
>
> *Guard them both at cost of life and limb*
>
> *I join my hands, beseeching you.*

Today, I join my hands, beseeching you to protect your minds. Be always mindful and introspective so that you will know yourself, so that you may live your life without fear, and live it with utmost authenticity.

Remember also Master Dogen's words:

> *To study the self is to forget the self*

To forget the self is to be enlightened by the ten thousand dharmas

To be enlightened by the ten thousand dharmas is to free one's body and mind to those of others

No trace of enlightenment remains, and this traceless enlightenment is continued forever

As we were reminded last time we met, to study oneself in this way requires an extraordinary amount of honesty and courage.

The Buddha teaches us that everything begins with the mind. In fact, he says is that everything **IS** just the mind. At least it is the conventional, every day mind that analyzes, separates, chooses what it likes and rejects what it dislikes. It is *this mind* that is the source of all of our stress and suffering. Every fear, anxiety, pain, pleasure, happiness, and joy all come from our minds. If you want to know yourself, if you want to really study yourself, then study your mind. Learn what it does and how it does it. Observe its every working. This is a very, very hard thing to do because we are, each and everyone of us, involved in a tricky, complicated love affair with our mind.

There is no greater love affair in our lives than the one we have with our mind. We believe that our thoughts are real. We believe that because, of course, everything that takes place in MY MIND is absolutely true, perceptive and perfect. This is the message we hear from our lover over and over again. Our lives are driven by this love affair. The mind is an extremely jealous lover. This lover can wrap us up and around almost anything it wants. It can do this because it has a voice that is beautiful, haunting, and so very, very persuasive. It is constantly whispering in our ears. It tells us, without pause or interruption, that WE are oh, so wonderful. It does its best to persuade us that everything it thinks, believes, feels, says, or does, and even things it can only imagine is wonderful. Because we don't know or understand this lover, we swoon under its spell. Should we catch ourselves falling into the spell and want to pull away, this lover will quickly shift our focus to some enticing distraction and we surrender. While each of us is enthralled with a highly developed and very personal lover, each one of them performs pretty much the same way.

`If we want to study ourselves we must delve deeply into the relationship we have with our lover. We must probe every aspect of our relationship. How do I choose to do or not something? Why do I think this way about this and that way about that? How often do I separate things into what I like or dislike? How many judgments and opinions do I make day in and day out? The answer to these questions shows us how we behave inside the confines of our love affair. Our relationship with this lover affects all our other relationships. This affair will take a toll on each of us and those around us. As you come to understand this love affair, you will find that your jealous lover is the provocateur of

As the story illustrates (and the Buddha teaches) we must begin with coming to a true knowledge of what is the best that we know about ourselves. After that comes the real challenge---living this best that we have come to know about US. How do we know what is the best about us? After all, isn't the thing that is "best" relative? We could spend a lot of time arguing about that, in fact we do all the time.

Have often have you thought or said, "I know what's best", but what you were really thinking is , "you're wrong and I'm right". The kind of knowing we are talking about here is knowing the self and knowing it intimately. This intimate knowledge is the threshold we must cross to truly live our lives. Isn't the only thing that matters that you choose what you believe is best, live that, and be tolerant and non-judgmental of those who chose differently? Ah, there's the other challenge---giving others the freedom to choose their own best even if it differs from yours. More about that challenge later. Just stick to finding your own truth first.

Because you are here in this Buddhist temple, I am also going to assume that each one of you has arrived at least these truths:

> The truth of stress and suffering and its causes: delusion, greed, and anger;

> There is a way to alleviate the stress and suffering and that is the Noble Eightfold Path;

> And, that love, compassion, sympathetic joy, and equanimity are the authentic results of our practice.

To live a Buddhist life to the fullest we must experience these three truths and cultivate them in our lives. This cultivation begins with this deep, intimate knowledge of self. Master Dogen in his <u>Shobogenzo Genjokoan, The Way of Everyday Life,</u> is very specific about the process of and the result of knowing the self. He says:

> *To study the Buddha Way is to study the self*

To study the self is to forget the self

To forget the self is to be enlightened by the ten thousand dharmas

To be enlightened by the ten thousand dharmas is to free one's body and mind to those of others

No trace of enlightenment remains, and this traceless enlightenment is continued forever

What he says is that before we can forget the self, we must study and know the self. He is saying that we must know ourselves intimately and honestly. Too often people jump to his conclusion---*forget the self*. They forget, or perhaps are afraid of the first part---*know the self*. It is impossible to forget the self until you have come to an honest, intimate knowledge of one's self. Also, notice that Master Dogen doesn't say we do this in isolation. Instead, he says that we can only come to know ourselves in relation to the ten thousand dharmas. What he means is that we can only come to know ourselves when we are immersed in all that is our life. We can never know ourselves by fleeing from it. Instead, we must live our lives fully, for that is where we come to face-to-face with ourselves. If we can achieve this knowledge of self and the forgetting of self, our enlightenment, as he says, continues forever.

To study oneself in this way requires an extraordinary amount of honesty. It also requires the courage to accept what we discover. We must be able to identify and understand everything about us: not just what we think, feel, or believe, but how those thoughts, feelings, and beliefs show up. We must look frankly at how we behave---our words, actions, tone of voice, body language, all the non-verbal cues we send that signal our attitude. We must stop completely any and all suggestion that the other person, thing, event, or idea is the source, cause, or blame of anything. We must embed in everything we think, feel, and do the Buddha's teaching that *we become what we think, feel, and do*. We must, without hesitation or excuse, know ourselves so intimately and honestly, that we should find ourselves sometimes leaping for joy and sometimes weeping in sadness. Until we do, we cannot know ourselves. Until we do, we cannot take up Master Dogen's challenge---to forget ourselves. In the final analysis, it is only in the forgetting of ourselves that we can arrive at the point of a *Lived Life*.

I believe with all my heart, that each person sitting here today wants more than anything to be able to say, every single day, "I am living life. I am living life with love, joy, compassion. I am living a life of purpose where I bring joy to one person in the morning and alleviate the suffering of one person in the afternoon. I am going to bed knowing that today, just like yesterday and hopefully tomorrow, I can say I lived".

This is the starting point in our creation of a *Lived Life*. We must begin with ourselves. We must have a frank, open, candid conversation with ourselves so that we can, at some point say, without any shadow of a doubt: I know myself. Then and only then, can we transcend ourselves, forget ourselves, and be a benefit to all beings. If we are able to summon the courage and muster the perseverance to eventually forget ourselves, we arrive at a place of utter bliss.

The Great Dharma King of the Three Realms, Je Tsongkhapa of the Tibetan tradition says this in his work, <u>The Twenty Seven Verses on Mind Training</u>:

> *Once identified with this luminous way of life, you will experience every moment as soaked in bliss., tasting the delight of compassionate responses to even the most negative actions of other beings. ... (and, sic) ... [we] remain intimate with the struggle of living beings as beacons of love and as the light of panoramic vision.*

Which one of us does not want a life of bliss? Who among us doesn't want to live a life of all of your thoughts and actions. This lover keeps you away from your true self; the self that is loving, kind, compassionate, happy, and joyful. On some level we all know this, yet, we find it extremely difficult to break our lover's spell. There will come a time, if you persist, when you will see the danger in this relationship. You will want to sever it. You will soon discover that it is a very hard thing to do. There is however, something that may help you. If we can keep this thing in sight it can assist and guide us in reducing our reliance on this lover affair---the law of *karma pitaka*.

Every thought, feeling, word, and deed we launch (karma) eventually has a consequence (pitaka). It may be today, tomorrow, next month, next year, or maybe our next lifetime, but have no doubt, the consequence will eventually result. This lover of ours ignores karma pitaka. This lover will work without pause to keep us from remembering the role karma pitaka plays in our lives. This lover of ours knows that if we are aware of how our actions play out and if we do our best to be mindful of their consequences, our lover no longer control us and it will fade away. Also know this for certain: this lover will fight and fight hard and dirty to keep us away from the truth of karma pitaka.

If we win, so to speak, and silence our lover, if we can remain ever mindful of our every thought, feeling, word, and deed, then something else happens. At first we might experience guilt, remorse, or shame. When these arise, our lover will see it as an opportunity and use all of its guile to get back with us. We must be vigilant when we reach this place.

What we must do when we reach this moment of potential reconciliation with our lover is quite specific: stop everything we are doing and atone for our past actions. Atonement is a way for us to tap into the memory of our past relationship with our lover. It helps to remind us of all the actions we have launched. It helps us to recall all of the consequences that flowed from our actions. It forces us to take stock of those that haven't manifested yet. Mostly importantly, taking the time to atone gives us a clear view of what our choice must be as our lover waits impatiently for us to return.

When we atone, we better have a clear idea of what we are atoning for otherwise the atonement is hallow. Knowing those things for which we want to atone is the first step along the path of studying ourselves, of getting to know ourselves, and our jealous lover. Engaging in atonement with candor and honesty, not hiding or holding back anything, gives us our first glimpse of freedom. It leads us to the happiness and joy that only a *Lived Life* can provide. Sometimes it can be difficult to face those things we want to atone for. Sometimes we aren't quite sure where to start. It may seem overwhelming to take inventory of our past actions let alone anticipate their consequences. Yet, if we want to engage a *Lived Life* we must. Fortunately, we don't have to rely just on our own devices, there is help.

Vashubandhu in his treatise, <u>Treasury of Knowledge</u>, says there are an infinite number of karmic actions and consequences each one of which flows from our body (actions), speech, and mind (thoughts and intentions). The <u>Lamrim Chenmo</u>, a Tibetan text, that in English is "Practicing the Path", takes Vashbandhu's work and organizes it into what it calls "The Ten Non-Virtues" that most of us can understand as producing negative karma. Each of these non-virtues is a hide-away where our lover wants to lure us. Our lover seduces us by whispering in our ear that WE are entitled to act in these non-virtuous ways. Our lover can be very persuasive in convincing us that we have nothing to atone for because we only are doing what we are entitled to do. We must not listen. This is one of the hardest things to overcome. Why? Because deep in the recesses of our deluded minds we actually do believe that we are entitled to act in these ways even when we know they will cause harm.

Let's remind ourselves of what they are. Then, when we begin our self-reflection at the end of this talk, you will have a sense of those things for which you want to atone. Perhaps you will also come to have a clearer view of how you behave when you are caught up in your love affair.

There are three non-virtues associated with the body:

Killing of a sentient being---Probably not much thought needed here

Stealing---Before you dismiss this one consider these forms of stealing: borrowing money with no intention to repay it, borrowing an item and not returning when you said you would, taking something because you thought the other person didn't need it as much as you do. How often have you acted in these ways?

Sexual misconduct---Here we must think in terms of exploitation, manipulation, and disrespect. For example, any relationship with someone already in a relationship is an inappropriate partner, someone who is subordinate to you, someone over whom you hold a special position, like a teacher and a student, forcing your partner into an unwanted encounter, sexual encounters that arise from anger, attachment, jealousy. Each of these are pitfalls that are easy to fall into in the heat of the moment.

There are four non-virtues associated with speech---this is an area we all have some work to do

Lying---Don't just think of the big lies, but remember that the little shadings of the truth that we think of as "white lies" are still lies. What about withholding then truth when speaking it is necessary for the benefit of the other person?

Divisive Speech---This is any speech that divides those who are in harmony. It includes any speech that intensifies an already tense situation, or interfering with reconciliations. If you are a member of a family, and most of us are, we have, at one time or another, either participated in or been the victim of divisive speech.

Harsh Speech---Here it's important to understand that it doesn't matter if the speech is true or not if the words carry ill-will. Any words that are harmful are wrong---period!

Gossip---Of all of the non-virtuous actions this is the one that we have all experience. It includes any speech that does not have a constructive and positive purpose. It includes not just the starting of gossip and rumor, but the repeating it, and even the enjoyment of it.

Vashibandhu also points out that there are three non-virtues of the mind:

A covetous mind---This is the desire to possess anything. This one is tricky. There are four aspects here:

1. attachment to your own things to the extent that you fear their loss or refuse to share them with others.
2. wanting the possessions of others whether it's their things, ideas, relationships. Think in terms of envy.
3. wanting the qualities or benefits of another. Again, think envy.
4. lack of a feeling of shame or remorse for your covetousness

Ill Will---This is another tricky one because there are aspects to this we may not consider. Wishing harm on another is the first aspect. It includes thinking over and over again how a person has hurt you until your anger arises. Ill will also includes the desire to retaliate. It includes even the thought of revenge.

Wrong view---The key here is exaggeration or making more of something than the facts support. Assuming what another thinks or feels and acting according to our assumptions is a good example. In fact, any thought that arises from ignorance, delusion, greed, anger is a wrong view.

Vashubandhu's list of non-virtuous actions are a way of taking inventory on how we behave sometimes. They remind us that once we put these non-virtues into action there will be consequences that affects us and others, not just in the moment, but sometimes well into our futures. As you take inventory of your actions don't just look at yourself. Look out and see all those who have been affected by your actions. Try to see how they have been harmed.

In taking this inventory we are studying ourselves just as Master Dogen suggests. We come to see our love affair exactly as it is with all of its nasty bits. What we see may help us learn to put an end to our affair, to forget ourselves, and live a life of ceaseless enlightenment and bliss.

Today we have begun the vigorous study of ourselves by facing the truth that we are in a complicated and harmful love affair. We started cleaning up the dirt and grime that is covering up the potential for a *Lived Life*. We do that by atoning for what we have already put in motion and the consequences flowing from them.

Before we begin our period of reflection, it is important that you understand why we say atone and not forgive. You must understand the difference between atoning for your past actions and seeking forgiveness for your past actions.

Some of your have heard this before: seeking forgiveness is just another act in support of your lover and yourself. Seeking forgiveness is a selfish act. Doesn't it take a lot of arrogance to ask those whom you have harmed to forgive you? You've already hurt them and now you want THEM to forgive YOU!! Somehow in asking for forgiveness we think WE are doing something quite special---admitting we were wrong. It's as if we are saying, "look at what a good person I am to admit that I harmed you. Isn't that wonderful of me! It's so great that you should forgive me." Can you hear how this is really all about you?

In our Buddhist practice we take a different view. Instead of seeking forgiveness, we engage in atonement. We come to that place where we ask nothing---we just give ourselves to the other acknowledging the hurt and harm we have caused. In atoning we admit, deeply, that we have caused harm. To those we have harmed---we ask absolutely nothing. We don't ask them to forgive us or understand us; we don't make excuses or diminish the impact or our actions. We accept that we have acted harmfully and express our remorse for having done so. And that is all. If we seek forgiveness or ask for understanding, if we make excuses or diminish in any way what we have done, we are not atoning at all. If we are listening to the voice of that lover telling us that what we did wasn't really all that bad, they'll get over it, we are lost in the love affair once more. Don't listen, atone.

As we contemplate atoning for our past actions, consider these words from The Rig Veda, a Hindu scripture:

If we have sinned against those who love us

Have wronged a brother, sister, dear friend, or a comrade

The neighbor of long standing or a stranger

Remove from us this stain

Reflection: Sit quietly. Read each of the following statements and pause for a few minutes between each one and observe what thoughts arise.

Let me look carefully at what I have done. Let me be diligent.

Have I made myself or others unhappy out of confusion, ignorance, greed, jealousy, pride, or anger?

(Silent reflection)

Have I made myself or others unhappy because of my craving, grasping or fear of letting go?

(Silent reflection)

Have I made myself or others unhappy because I put my needs above those of others?

(Silent reflection)

Once you have finished the silent reflection recite the following:

Today I begin anew to purify and free my heart with awakened wisdom, bright as the sun and the full moon, and with immeasurable compassion to help humankind.

With the torch of wisdom, I leave behind the forest of confusion.

With determination, I will learn, reflect, and practice.

I will do my best to abide in the Noble Eightfold Path that is the ground for all my intentions and actions.

Whenever anger or anxiety enters my heart, I will return to my breath, which is the safe harbor of mindfulness.

May I bring feelings of peace and joy into every household.

May I plant wholesome seeds on the ten thousand paths.

May I never attempt to escape the suffering of the world, but always remain present whenever beings need my help.

Where is the Mind? What is myself?

So far we have explored our fear of a *Lived Life*, the tortured love affair we have with our own minds, and taken the time to atone for our past harmful thoughts, words, and actions. What we have been doing is studying ourselves as closely as we can so that we begin to forget ourselves and engage a *Lived Life*. Now, we must dig a little deeper. Now, we must take a sharp, penetrating look at what we call mind and self. It is a deeper and more penetrating look at the lover we talked about the last time we met. What we will discover is that you and your lover (the self/mind) aren't really separate. What you may find is that they are like conjoined twins--- separate yet intricately intertwined.

Let us begin with a passage from the Hsin Hsin Ming written in the Sixth Century by the Third Zen patriarch, Seng-t'san. If you want to read one text that will convey to you the essence of the relationship between truth, self, and mind study the <u>Hsin Hsin Ming</u>. It is where we begin today:

> *If you wish to know the truth,*
>
> *Then hold no opinion for or against anything.*
>
> *To set up what you like against what you dislike*
>
> *Is the disease of the mind.*
>
> *Indeed, it is due to our grasping and rejecting*
>
> *That we do not know the true nature of things.*
>
> *Live neither in the entanglements of outer things,*
>
> *Nor in ideas or feelings of emptiness.*
>
> *Be serene and at one with things*
>
> *And erroneous views will disappear by themselves. ...*

> *When the mind exists undisturbed in The Way,*
>
> *There is no objection to anything in the world;*
>
> *And when there is no objection to anything*
>
> *Things cease to exist in the old way...*
>
> *When in harmony with the nature of things, your own fundamental nature,*
>
> *You will walk freely and undisturbed.*

"To walk freely and undisturbed in harmony with your own fundamental nature.," that, my friends, is liberation. Walking freely and undisturbed IS the way of a *Lived Life*. Why isn't it easy? As Master Seng-t'san reminds us, it is because of our incessant separating what we like from what we don't like. It is difficult for us because we can't help but listen to the seductive voice of our lover who is petrified of being left behind by us.

We must, if we want a *Lived Life* that is free and undisturbed, to become intimate with that which keeps us from having such a life and that thing is our mind. Starting today we should re-imagine our lover as simply our mind. After all, it is the mind that gives birth to the lover. Our mind wants us to see the world in terms of subjects and objects to grasp at or reject. It is the mind that mostly sees us as the subject and everything else as an object to be possessed or discarded by us. It is this discriminating mind that we must become intimate with because it is the creator of self, the I, me, and mine, of our existence. Until we do, there is no hope of forgetting the self and being liberated from it.

Just as we took an honest inventory of our past actions for which we wanted to atone, we must now take an even franker look at the relationship between mind and self. We must come to know what they are so that we can live our lives fully and authentically.

Where are these things we call mind and self? Do we have more than one mind or self? How do we know which one is the true mind or the true self? It is these questions that are at the root of our practice. We must know not just our true mind and self, but the false mind and the false selves that we have created as well.

The reading from the HSin Hisn Ming is a good place to start because it points us to the fundamental activity of the mind and the selves we create: separating what we like from what we dislike and clinging to what we like and rejecting what we don't like. That's the root of our stress and suffering. Who or what does this separating? Our mind and our self, the conjoined twins. Nothing else. So, to know the self is to know the mind; to know the mind is to know the self.

Where is this mind/self? Can you locate it? We know where the brain is, but where is the mind/self? When does the mind/self awaken? Does a fetus have a mind/self; a new born?

When does the mind/self start to shut down? Are people with dementia or Alzheimer's disease losing their mind/self? If the mind/self has a location, then we should be able to show it to another person, to touch it, display it for others to see. But, we can't. Where is the mind/self? All of Buddha's teachings, one might argue, are about answering this question.

Before we get to the Buddha's teachings on mind/self, let's consider this observation from Antonio Damasio in his book, <u>Self Comes to Mind</u>:

> *The fact that no one can see the minds of others, conscious or not, is especially mysterious. We can observe their bodies and their actions, what they do or say or write, and we can make informed guesses about what they think. But we cannot observe their minds and only we can observe ours, from the inside, and through a rather narrow window.. The properties of minds, let alone conscious minds, appear to*

be so radically different from those of visible living matter that thoughtful people wonder how one process (conscious minds working) meshes with other processes (physical cells living together in aggregates called organs).

What is interesting about what he says is that he is raising the question of what and where is the mind. Ananda posed this same question to the Buddha. The Buddha's answer is laid out in detail in the <u>Surangama Sutra</u>. In the sutra t he Buddha explains the Five Aggregates or Skandhas to Ananda. This is the process whereby the mind gives rise to the self. Did you notice that Damasio also uses the idea of aggregates (cells) coming together to create the organs giving rise to consciousness? As we will see shortly, the Buddha's explanation of self rests squarely on our sensory experience of six sense organs: eye, ear, nose, tongue, body, and mind. It seems Damasio didn't really discover anything all that new, but re-states, in contemporary terms, the idea of the Five Aggregates or Skandhas.

In the <u>Surangama Sutra</u>, the Buddha and Ananda engage in a lengthy discourse on the mind. This sutra is as important for the Hua Yen and Zen schools in China and Korea as the Avatamsaka and Lotus Sutras. It roughly translates as the "Sutra on the Indestructible". I suppose we could say it is a sutra on the indestructibility of the mind---but, which mind is that; is it the everyday mind or the true mind? Is it the mind that creates the self or the mind before self? That is for you to discover. Approximately 400 pages of the sutra are devoted to an exploration of the mind. The rest of the sutra is devoted to specific contemplations and practices.

In the second chapter, entitled 'The Location of the Mind", Ananda proposes seven possible locations for the mind. The Buddha responds to each of Ananda's suggestions by pointing out that what he thinks is his mind is nothing more than a mental process. He says that he mistakes this process for the mind itself and that he accepts this mental process as proof of self. All of it is a grand and expansive delusion.

Does the Buddha give Ananda directions to the location of the mind? Not exactly. What he does is distill that process to what we call the Skandhas, or The Five Aggregates. For us westerners The Five Aggregates may be easier to understand than Skandhas. An aggregate is a collection of elements that come together to form a whole. In our belief system the Five Aggregates, or elements, come together to form the whole we call self.

The Buddha's root teaching on the mind, the self, stress and suffering all arise out of his penetration of the process of the Five Aggregates. In Division 1 of the *Khandhavagga* of the Samyutta Nikaya he teaches:

> *How, householder, is one afflicted in body and afflicted in mind? ... He regards form as self or self as possessing form. He lives*

> *possessed by the notions, "I am form, form is mine". As he lives obsessed by these notions, that form of his changes and alters. With the change and alteration of the form there arises in him sorrow, lamentation, pain, displeasure, and despair. (the same is true when he...)regards feeling, perception, volitional acts, consciousness as self.*

These Aggregates give rise to the illusion of self and when this self is faced with the reality of impermanence it wants to flee from this truth. Yet, if we want to embrace a *Lived Life*, if we want to know this thing called self, if we want to transcend it so that we live authentically, then we must understand how these Five Aggregates work.

A preliminary word or two: this entire process, in fact all that we experience, comes to us through only six gates or entrances --- the senses (sight, sound, smell, taste, touch, thought). There are no experiences other than these. So, as we discuss the Five Aggregates keep this mind.

While that this process occurs in steps, they happen so rapidly and are so dynamic and fluid that they happen almost simultaneously. As we mature and our experiences of the world increase, the rapidity with which this process unfolds is beyond the measure of time.

There are five aggregates or elements: form, perception, feeling, volition, and consciousness. Even thought they are a dynamic process, for our purposes today let's take them one at a time.

The process begins with form. We encounter the world via objects we call form. These are people, things, places, or ideas. They come into the world because certain causes and conditions have come together to bring them into existence. The moment they come into existence they are beginning to alter and change into something else. This is our first delusion--- we fail to understand this. We are unable or unwilling to face the fact that virtually everything is morphing into something else the very second it comes into existence. This thing we call self refuses to accept the transitory and impermanent nature of all things. It refuses because if it accepts the impermanence of just one thing, then it must also accept that it too is impermanent.

We also fail to understand that, in and of themselves, not one of these forms has any quality or value. We assign value to them later. Once we come in contact with a person, place, thing, or idea we perceive it. In other words, we become aware of it.

This perception/awareness is bare perception. Think of it this way. Just around the corner, in the next room, is a coffee cup. Then, you step around the corner and see it. This immediate "seeing" is bare awareness. You haven't yet formed any opinion about it. Or, someone is cooking in the basement and what they are cooking is very aromatic, but the aroma has not reached us up here yet. Someone opens the door to the basement and the smell fills the room and you notice it. That is what we mean by bare perception or awareness. It is the awareness of something before we layer on all of judgments and evaluations about it and before we decide to cling to it or grab hold of it so that we can throw it away.

Once we have become barely aware of the form we immediately begin to give it value. We pull up any experienes we may we have with this person, place, thing, or idea and any even remotely similar experiences. We formulate feelings about this person, place, thing, or idea. We are so good at this part of the process that, if we could stand aside and watch ourselves, we would see that we concoct elaborate stories about these forms none of which are true. Our stories lead us to one of two conclusions: we either like it or we dislike it. We may say that we are ambivalent sometimes, but if we look deeper we can always find an acceptance or rejection.

Once we have decided whether we like or dislike something, we then decide to (this is the volitional part) to either cling to the things we like or reject and throw away those we dislike. Volitional here means the act of choosing. This is not the decision to like or dislike, this is the decision to accept or reject; this is the decision that says, "I want this and will have it, or, I hate this and it needs to be cast aside".

The next part of the process is consciousness. Consciousness in means YOUR TOTAL AWARENESS of the form, your feelings, your emotions, and your decisions about this person, place, thing, or idea. Where perception is a bare awareness before picking and choosing, consciousness is an awareness that is based solely on YOU---all of your stories about the person, place, thing, or idea. It includes every assumption you make, every prediction you hold. It is this consciousness that is at the root of all of your stress and suffering. If you could really step aside and observe yourself you would be shocked at how much of your day is spent swirling inside this process of the Five Aggregates. It is about the only thing we do all day long. Then, we put the final touch on it all by believing beyond any shadow of a doubt that our current consciousness rests in absolute, unadulterated truth.

Stop to consider for a moment that my consciousness of a particular person, place, thing, or idea may not be the same as yours because my feelings and decisions about it are different. The person next to you, behind you, in front of you all may have a different consciousness about it as well. We must then ask ourselves: whose consciousness abides in truth? Or, perhaps there is no truth, just different experiences and consciousness. Those differences are evidence of two things: the mind and the self. One, the mind, we can't seem to locate, and the second, the self, doesn't exist at all. The only thing we know for sure is the workings of the Five Aggregates and, because they give rise to self, they are the ground of ignorance, greed, and anger. They are the roots of all stress and suffering. They create I, me, and mine. Your "I-ness" is not my "I-ness" yet we cling to the delusion that our individual truth is the only truth. When we can truly understand the truth of the process of the Five Aggregates then we can begin to see why things in the world are the way they are.

This brings us back to Buddha and Master Seng-t'san. The Five Aggregates are the great facilitators of our grasping and rejecting which are, in turn, the catalysts for the separating disease of the mind. When we are plagued by this disease, we suffer sorrow, lamentation, pain, displeasure, and despair. Yes, they can also lead to pleasure, but that too is impermanent and only leads us to more grasping and clinging and thus more stress and suffering.

Today we are asked to become aware and mindful of the Five Aggregates. This process can be of tremendous help to us in getting to know how this thing we call self comes about. The more we come to know how the Five Aggregates work, the closer we come to knowing ourself so that someday, if even for a few moments, we can say, "I forgot myself." When we penetrate the mind as self, when we appreciate the process of the Five Aggregates, we have completed laying the foundation for a *Lived Life*. From this point forward we will begin the task of building a structure of a *Lived Life* on this foundation.

Reflection:

I'd like to suggest that you hold a two-sentence phrase on each out breath you take.

One the first out breath ask this question: *what am I?*

On the next out breath you answer the question this way: *I don't know.*

Keep repeating this two breath cycle of question and answer and observe what shows up for you. No matter what does show up, don't chase it, don't try to understand it, don't analyze or evaluate it. Just note it and keep posing the question and answer.

Compassion

Let's begin today by pausing for just a moment to appreciate the work we have done so far in laying the foundation for a *Lived Life*. We have acknowledged that we have a fundamental fear of living a fully engaged life. We have atoned for our past thoughts, words, and actions. We have come to understand that our minds are the source of our suffering and that it is our minds that keep us from living our lives to the fullest. We have come to understand that there is a process called the Five Aggregates with which we create this thing called self and that this self is relentless in pursuing what it likes and rejecting what it doesn't. Having experienced what we have so far, we are now eager to move through our former selves so that we can be fully present, engaged, and living life. This is a very good place to be. We could not be here if we had not explored what we have the past several weeks. Let's now begin the construction of a *Lived Life.*

Korean Zen poet Jungkwan Haean wrote:

The man who is free and easy

Beyond every boundary, is enlightened,

He doesn't hoe much,

But there are no weeds in his field.

These verses remind us that no matter how free and easy we are, no matter how enlightened, even when we don't see any weeds cluttering out minds, we must still keep vigilant to pull the weeds as soon as they sprout. It's good to be reminded of this from time to time. However, let's focus more on the free and easy part he speaks about in the first line. He says that a free and easy person is enlightened. Let's change that word 'enlightened' to the word 'liberated'. The word enlightened has been overused and little understood so let's stick with liberated. 'Liberated' keeps us more grounded and avoids all the pre-conceived notions we carry about enlightenment.

The person who is free and easy is liberated! Are you free and easy? Do you want to be free and easy? Stupid question! Of course you do. Isn't that why you are here---seeking a way to freedom and ease? To move freely and at ease you must engage a Liv*ed Life*; one that is authentic and fearless.

How to engage a *Lived Life*? That's the real question isn't it?

When we come to those points in our life when we want to make changes we often look to role models for the things we want to bring into our life. We want to be able to examine these role models, see how they think. We want to witness the way they behave so that we can emulate them. We look for those who, in short, live the very way we want to live. We are very fortunate in our tradition to have just such role models available to us. We can rely on them as exemplars of a *Lived Life* and employ them as the building materials for a *Lived Life*. We don't have to seek them out. They are already here and present for us if we want them to be.

While there are many Buddhist personages to whom we can look to as exemplary persons who have lived fully engaged lives, we are going to focus on just four of them. Each one of them is a bodhisattva. A bodhisattva is an enlightened, liberated being who has made a conscious decision to remain in the cycle of birth and death from one life to the next so that they can work ceaselessly for the enlightenment and liberation of everyone. Their commitment is so strong that they will continue successive lives until everyone is liberated. That should strike you as both extraordinary and nearly impossible to achieve. However, if they are undaunted shouldn't we be too?

The four bodhisattvas to whom we will look as role models for a *Lived Life* each represent a very specific aspect of such a life. If we can bring each of these aspects into our lives not only will we be fully engaged in living authentically, we will be liberated. From our liberation we will be able to bring joy and happiness into this world.

The four bodhisattvas are: Avalokiteshvara or Kuan Yin, Manjushri, Samantabhadhra, and Khsitigarbha. We will devote one week to each of them so that we can come to know them well. Today, we begin by getting to know the Bodhisattva of Great Compassion.

Who is this Bodhisattva of Great Compassion? Unlike the other Bodhisattvas, the Bodhisattva of Great Compassion is represented as both a male, Avalokiteshvara, and a female, Kuan Yin (Guanyin in China). Over time, Kuan Yin, the female aspect of this bodhisattva, has taken precedence in terms of representations (see our two statues, yet a separate altar to Kuan Yin), and object of contemplation. She is of special focus and attention in Tibetan, Chinese, Japanese, and Korean Buddhism. Together with her male aspect, this Bodhisattva of Great Compassion is the most widely revered of all the Bodhisattvas and one of the earliest to appear in Buddhist literature. This might be because compassion is the well-spring of all the other aspects of the Bodhisattva ideal. It is the well-spring of a *Lived Life*.

As we begin to think about the importance of Compassion in a *Lived Life*, consider this: Charles Darwin concluded that compassion and kindness are necessary for survival. This is a pretty profound statement from the father of evolutionary theory. He says that we cannot survive without compassion and kindness yet how often have you heard this said about evolution? We should also stop to consider that compassion and kindness are not things that come to us late in life. Recent research has shown that infants begin to show compassionate and kind behaviors as early as 18 months. If we develop these traits this early age why does it seem the world is so lacking in them? What happens to us? Where does our kindness and compassion go? I'm not suggesting that they become forever lost. They just are misplaced and can be difficult to re-discover. But, if we want a fully engaged, authentic, liberated life, we must find them and return them to a place of prominence on our lives. Kuan Yin can lead us back to them. She can show us how to live them.

What does Kuan Yin teach us? What is it that we must we learn from her? A very good answer to these questions can be found in the "Invocation of the Bodhisattvas" that appears on p. 25 of the Ritual and Practices book. Let's turn to that page and read the invocation together.

> *I invoke your name, Kuan Yin/Avalokiteshvara. I aspire to learn your way of listening in order to help relieve the suffering in the world. You know how to listen in order to understand. I invoke your name in order to practice listening with all my intention and open-heartedness. I will sit and listen without prejudice. I will sit*

and listen without judging or reacting. I will sit and listen in order to understand. I will sit and listen so attentively that I will be able to hear what the other person is saying and also what is being left unsaid. I know that just by listening deeply I already alleviate a great deal of pain and suffering in the other person.

What we learn from this invocation is that her way of compassionately engaging with living beings is to listen. Not to speak, not to act, not to intercede; just to listen. How many of us think that just listening is an act of compassion? How many of us have said to ourselves, "I need to listen more than I do"?

This isn't a very easy thing to do---just listen. In the recitation we learn that Kuan Yin doesn't listen the way most of us do. She has a very particular way of listening. It is one that we may find easy to understand, but a challenge to engage.

Research shows that most of us don't really listen like Kuan Yin at all. We listen so we can respond instead of listening so we can understand. Let's hear that again: *most of us listen so we can respond rather than listening so we can understand*. This is important. We mostly listen so that we can respond. Why is this so important? It's important because when we can shift from listening so that we can respond to listening as Kuan Yin does (to understand), we become focused on the other person rather than ourselves. When we listen in the old way (so that we can respond) we are listening so that we can advance our own ideas, our own opinions, our own observations, the way we think things ought to be, etc., etc.. Kuan Yin's compassionate way of listening manifests itself in listening in a deeply connected, attentive way without any of our own thoughts, ideas, opinions, or observation.

In the recitation we learn that Kuan Yin's way of listening requires open-heartedness and the intention to understand. She listens to understand both what is being said and what is not being said. She listens without prejudice, judgment, or reaction. This is where the challenge for us arises: to listen without prejudice, judgment or reaction. If there is one thing that is the hardest for us to do it is to listen without reaction or judgment. In fact, if you are paying attention you are probably reacting and judging this very statement!

To listen whole-heartedly one MUST listen without prejudice, judgment, or reaction. When one listens *in this way* it can be a moment of liberation and enlightenment. When we listen *in this way*, we experience the other just as they are. We see them clearly just as they are *in this moment*. If we can do this, then we can, as the recitation says, alleviate a great deal of pain and suffering in the other person.

We must ask ourselves: have I ever considered that listening in this way is a deep way of expressing compassion? We should also ask ourselves: how often do I listen in this way?

If we want to engage a *Lived Life*, to live a life or freedom and ease, this is the place to start. Develop the art of listening in the way Kuan Yin/Avalokitesevara does.

I'd like to make one additional suggestion. So far we've talked about listening to the other. Perhaps we should extend that same deep, open-hearted, attentive, non-judgmental listening to ourselves. It might be a way to alleviate some of our own pain and suffering.

You may be asking yourself at this point, "if I can do this, then what happens? Not just to the other person, but, if I develop this as a wholesome habit, a kind of virtuous conduct, what are the effects"?

Nagarjuna, the third century CE Indian Buddhist philosopher, in his work, <u>The Treatise on the Provisions for Enlightenment</u>, describes the effects of Great Compassion this way:

> *The great compassion penetrates to the marrow of one's bones.*

Thus one serves as a refuge for every being.

With a feeling as strong as a father's regard for his only son,

One's kindness extends universally to all beings.

How right he was!

In 2012 three psychology researchers at Stanford University's center for the Study of Compassion and Altruism, in an article entitled, "Social Connection and Compassion: Important Predictors of Health and Well-Being", reported the results of their fMRI (Functional MRI) studies. What they found is that when the brain is activated by compassion---*an other oriented emotion*---it was associated with the empathy network {of the brain}, the region of the brain responsible for the sensation of pain and the perception of other's pain, as well as parental nurturing behaviors. I wonder if these researchers are aware that they have just proved what Nagarjuna knew almost 2000 years ago.

The act of deep, attentive listening, this act of Great Compassion, if we choose to practice it, penetrates into every aspect of our being. We become a place of safety and refuge for others. This is an extraordinary place to create. It is a place of liberation and ease. Liberation and ease: the ground on which to build a *Lived Life*. If we live a life of Great Compassion it penetrates to the very marrow of our bones. This is what the Bodhisattva Kuan Yin/Avalokitesevara has to teach us about a *Lived Life*. Our challenge now is to go and engage it!

Reflection:

This week try reciting the following "song" each day. Observe your thoughts and feelings as you do. Look for changes in how you move through your day and engage with others. Where do you find ease and where do you find difficulty.

The Song of Compassion

My heart goes out to all those who are now suffering, my very own mothers who have cared for me so kindly, throughout the whole of time, from its very beginnings until now.

These kind mothers of mine helped to cool me when I was hot, but now some have taken birth in the eight hot hells to be tormented by the searing heat —my heart goes out to them!

These mothers of mine gave me warmth when I was cold, but now some have taken birth in the eight cold hells to be tormented by the freezing cold —my heart goes out to them!

These mothers of mine gave me food and drink in my hunger and thirst, but now some have taken birth in the preta realm

to be tormented by famine and drought
—my heart goes out to them!

These kind mothers of mine always cared for me with love, but now some have taken birth among the animals to be tormented by servitude and exploitation —my heart goes out to them!

These kind mothers of mine lovingly gave me whatever I desired, but now some have taken birth among human beings to be tormented by the pains of aging and death —my heart goes out to them!

These kind mothers of mine shielded me from every harm, but now some have taken birth among the asuras to be tormented by conflict and strife —my heart goes out to them!

These kind mothers of mine nurtured me and brought me only benefit, but now some have taken birth among the gods To be tormented by death and transmigration —my heart goes out to them!

By ourselves, we have no chance to escape samsara's pains,
And for now you lack the power to provide your own protection—
O my mothers, undergoing all this suffering, my heart goes out to you!

When I consider these sufferings which we all endure, I think to myself, 'If only I could gain enlightenment! Let it not be tomorrow,
but let it come to me today!'

Swiftly, ever so swiftly, may I gain awakening, and, having done so, dispel all beings' pain, leading them all to perfect bliss, I pray!

Understanding and Wisdom

Let's begin today by listening to the words from the seventeenth century Chinese sage, Hung Ying-ming:

In establishing yourself in life

If you do not raise yourself at least one step higher,

It will be like shaking off your clothes in a dust cloud,

Like washing your feet in the mud.

How will you ever excel?

In living in the world, if you do not step back a single pace for others,

You will be like the moth that hurls itself into the lamp,

Or the ram that catches its horns in the hedge.

How will you ever be at peace?

Master Hung Ying-ming paints a simple picture of what we must do to raise ourselves above the fray of our lives so that we can be at peace. Notice that he ties our personal peace to that of others when he says, "step back a single step for others". If you understand what he is saying then you understand that a *Lived Life* is the life of the bodhisattva. A *Lived Life* is one lived for the liberation of everyone, not just those that are easy to live for or those closest to you. The life of a bodhisattva is a challenge. The life off the bodhisattva is, however, an authentically *Lived Life*.

Last time we were together we came to know Kuan Yin, the Bodhisattva of Great Compassion. We came to learn that she teaches us the primary way of engaging a *Lived Life*: we must listen. We must listen to what is being said and what is not being said. We must listen attentively, wholeheartedly, and without hesitation or judgment. We must listen to everything this way. It is the wellspring of compassion and the source of a Liv*ed Life*. It is the threshold of being at peace.

If compassionate, unconditional listening is the foundation of a *Lived Life*, what is the pinnacle of a *Lived Life*? What is it that permeates and pervades a *Lived Life* if we are able to master this particular, all pervasive skill? Who is it, which bodhisattva, teaches us this way of being? What skill does he teach? Does this skill raise us one step higher while taking one step back? Does it lead to a life of peace? This short answer to these questions is yes. Our next bodhisattva model teaches us about being still and understanding. He is the perfect compliment to listening.

I like to think of the Bodhisattva of Great Compassion, Kuan Yin, and the Bodhisattva of Understanding and Wisdom as being like bookends. Between them align the other skills of a *Lived Life*. Together, they hold a Lived Life together and together they lead to freedom, ease, and peace. I'm talking about the bodhisattva Manjushri.

Understanding what Manjushri can teach is a bit tricky. The recitation associated with his name is the shortest of the ones we will examine and seems quite straightforward. The invocation of Manjushri tells us that the skill he models for us is, *"to be still and look deeply into the heart of things and into the hearts of people . . . I will look deeply so that I will be able to see and understand the roots of suffering, the impermanent and selfless nature of all that is"*. On the surface it seems much like what we learned from Kuan Yin about listening. But when Manjushri speaks to us about looking what are we suppose to look with? Which "eyes" are we suppose to use to look? What are we looking for? Let's begin with the last question first: what are we looking for?

As he teaches us, we are looking for the root of suffering in the person who stands before us. To do this we must be still. Not just physically still, but our minds and hearts must be still. All of OUR perceptions and judgments must be stilled. Our ego must be quieted. Unless we can be this still, what we see in the other is is obscured by our own agenda. We will not be able to see *their suffering* . We must cut off all thinking that has us at its center. It is why Manjushri is depicted with a sword in his hand. He wields the sword that cuts through ignorance and cuts off the ego. Just as every Buddha and bodhisattva is already present in us, we also already possess Manjushri's sword. We just need to keep it honed and ready to use. Manjushri's cutting off is just this: cut off all ego attachments and stop all that flows from them. Still them, quiet them, and then, and only then, will you will be ready to look.

Once we have become still and quiet, he teaches us to look. But he doesn't want us to look with our ordinary eyes. He wants us to look with the eyes of wisdom, the eyes of *prajna*. Why the eyes of wisdom; because these are the eyes that see, as the recitation says, "the roots of suffering, the impermanent and selfless nature of all that is". These are the eyes that have penetrated the teachings on impermanence, suffering, selfishness, and self-less-ness. Until we have attained this kind of clarity of vision, it doesn't matter how much we have stopped and stilled ourselves, we won't be able to see wholeheartedly into the heart and suffering of those before us and this is precisely the thing we must see if we are to engage a *Lived Life*.

Manjushri also teaches us that to gain the wisdom of the Buddha's teachings we must embed them in our lives. It is why he is depicted holding a text of the teachings in his other hand. With the teachings in one hand and the sword that cuts off ignorance in the other, we can begin to be still and look wholeheartedly into things as they are.

There is still more we learn from Manjushri's experiences that lead to wisdom. These are practices, behaviors if you will, that in and of themselves lead to wisdom, understanding, and prompt compassion. One particular experience he had was a teaching given directly to Manjushri by the Buddha himself in chapter 14 of the <u>Lotus Sutra</u> entitled, "Safe and Easy Practices". We too must learn these safe and easy practices if we are to fully engage a *Lived Life*.

Chapter 14 begins with Manjushri being described by the Buddha as, "the great one, prince of the Dharma" to demonstrate the depths of Manjushri's understanding of the teachings and his attainment of the ideal of the bodhisattva life yet, even Manjushri needs to learn more. The Buddha points out that he must engage in some very specific practices each of which leads to understanding and wisdom. Here is what the Buddha teaches Manjushri:

> *Manjushri, what do I mean by the practices of bodhisattva great ones? If a bodhisattva great one is always patient, is gentle and agreeable, is never violent, and never gets alarmed, and if, moreover, such a*

bodhisattva does not act in such a way s to become attached to anything, but perceives the nature of the reality of all things, not acting, not discriminating---this is what I call the practices of the bodhisattva great ones.

If we look at these closely, we can see that the Buddha is pointing out to Manjushri that these practices point head towards stillness and listening. Patient, gentle, agreeable, never violent, never alarmed: each of these is a practice of stillness. Our minds, hearts, and bodies are never agitated or noisy when we are patient, gentle, agreeable, and not violent or alarmed. If we take just a minute to think about this, we have a clear view of a path toward the stillness that allows us to both listen and understand. Let's hear them again, this time a little slower so that we allow them to sink in: patient, gentle, agreeable, never violent, never alarmed.

The other practice the Buddha points to is the practice of understanding: perceive the nature of the reality of all things without attaching to them or discriminating among them. When we understand in this way we come to accept things as they are. When we are still and listen attentively and wholeheartedly we can penetrate the suffering of others. We can experience the pain caused by their clinging and grasping. We can understand their fear. When we come to understand these things about them, then we arrive at a place where compassion for them flows easily and naturally. Our compassion flows out without limit or boundary. It flows without any trace of "me".

Kuan Yin and Manjushri---the bookends of a L*ived Life.* They teach us that a *Lived Life* is a life where we dwell in each moment quiet and still, listening to what is being said and what is not being said so that we can understand the roots of suffering in ourselves and those whom we encounter day-to-day. When we live our life in this way we arrive at a place of ease and peace. Arriving here we can live a life where, as the ancient Chinese philosopher Hung Ying-ming said:

> *When you have broken through the secrets*
> *lying right before your eyes*
>
> *One thousand heroes of old will be*
> *delivered to your grasp.*

Reflection:

Sit silently and reflect one ach of the following questions. Read each one to yourself and then send a few minutes reflecting on the question. Pay close attention to how you respond to each one.

1. How do I behave when I'm impatient?
2. How do I behave when I'm being patient?
3. Do I consider myself to be a gentle person?
4. Would most people say I am agreeable or disagreeable?

5. Have I ever been violent in any way, physically, emotionally, psychologically?
6. Do I become easily alarmed?
7. Where would I like to improve? Patience? Agreeability? Gentleness? What else?

Joy in Action

You know how sometimes when you are cooking something and you have followed the recipe exactly, then you taste it. It tastes sort of okay. You say to yourself, "it needs something". You might even ask someone else, "I think it needs something, what do you think?". You may add a pinch of salt or a little more pepper. You taste it and then you say, "ah, that's just what it needed". You make a note in the margin of the cook book to add more salt next time. It's not there is anything wrong with the recipe, it was that YOU KNEW it needed something else to make it just right. It just needed a pinch of this or that to balance out the flavors.

We are following the recipe of an engaged, authentic, *Lived Life*. So far we have added together compassionate listening, wise and understanding looking, stirred in wholeheartedness and added a healthy portion of attentiveness. As we taste what we've mixed so far, we find that it tastes pretty good, but it's not quite what we want just yet. Today we will add not just a pinch of something, but a strong dose of it.

Let's go back to our recipe book, the Rituals and Practices book, page 26. There we find the ingredient we need. This Bodhisattva actually sounds like an exotic ingredient: Samantabadhra. Samantabadhra, if we say it a few times it begins to sound just like an exotic herb or spice that will enliven our recipe and bring a little spice to it. Today, the Bodhisattva we are going to come to know is just like the added pinch of salt to our recipe. He is going to provide the balance we need to truly live our lives. Let's read the invocation of Samantabadhra, together:

> *I invoke your name, Samantabadhra. I aspire to practice your vow to act with eyes and heart of compassion, to bring joy to one person in the morning and joy to one person in the afternoon. I know that the*

happiness of others is my own happiness, and I aspire to practice joy on the path of service. I know that every word, every look, every action, and every smile can bring happiness to others. I know that if I practice wholeheartedly, I myself may become an inexhaustible source of peace and joy for my loved ones and for all species.

What is the essence of this ingredient, Samantabahdra? Where Kuan Yin was the essence of looking and Manjushri was the essence of looking, Samantabadhra is the essence of action. Just like the Bodhisattvas that we looked at before, it's not just any kind of acting. It is quite a specific kind of action. It is acting with joy. Maybe a better way to say it is: Joy in Action. It's not just the feeling of joy, but putting joy into action. It is also an attitude. It is attitude towards joy that manifests in our actions.

Before we look closely at Joy in Action, let's listen to what the Buddha had to say about Samatabahdra:

> *The Bodhisattva of Great Conduct is called Universal Worthy.*
>
> *The sea of his vow power is multilayered without bounds.*
>
> *By wisdom he is born.*
>
> *His originally wonderful virtue is pervasive and perfected.*
>
> *His efficacious response and spiritual power shake the great thousand realms.*
>
> *Homage to the Bodhisattva of Great Conduct.*

That's quite a statement of respect. Think about what the Buddha said. This Bodhisattva's vow of Great Conduct is pervasive and perfected and shakes every realm. What the Buddha points us to is ths: if we too can take up the vow of Joy in Action, we too can shake every realm of our life. There are several other names Samatabahdra is called all of which point us in different ways to the impact of Joy in Action. He is also known as: The Bodhisattva Universal Good, the Bodhisattva of Never Disparaging, the Bodhisattva of Never Underestimating Living Beings, and Forest of Virtues Bodhisattva. These are powerful names. Each one of them reminds us of how we should act: good, virtuous, never disparaging or underestimating another person. Remember also that it's not just our actions, but our intentions as well.

There is also a short description given by the Buddha about how Samantabahdra spent his days which serves as an inspiration for all of us:

> *The monk did not devote himself to reading and reciting sutras, but simply went around bowing to people. If he saw groups off in the distance he would make a point of going up to them and bowing and*

praising them saying, 'I would never dare to disrespect you, because surely you are all to become buddhas.

I'm not sure how such conduct would be received in our culture, but the idea of approaching everyone with decency and respect is the point. If we can act in these ways then we are a source of joy.

Joy means such things as:

> Delight, great pleasure, joyfulness, jubilation, exultation, rejoicing, happiness, gladness, glee, exhilaration, exuberance, elation, euphoria, bliss, ecstasy, rapture, felicity

All of these meanings are active. Glee, exuberance, jubilation, for example, are words that suggest things like skipping, dancing, singing. Joy in action is not something you do by sitting in a corner and thinking or reading about it. It is something you DO. And here's the important part---you don't do it alone; you do it with and for others.

What then is Samantabahdra teaching us about joy in action? First, and maybe foremost, he teaches us that if we can combine joy in action with compassionate listening and wise and understanding looking, we become an inexhaustible source of not just joy, but peace as well. He also teaches HOW to do this: "*know that every word, every look, every action, and every smile can bring happiness to others.*"

Every word, every look, every action, and especially the act of smiling, are the places we must focus our wholehearted attention when putting Joy into Action. This asks a great deal of us doesn't it? It might even sound overwhelming. You might be thinking, "I'm suppose to make everything I do joyful? Who does that?" No one is suggesting that if you can't do this all the time that you are falling short. The lesson these bodhisattvas teach us is to try, try our best, try wholeheartedly, and try as attentively as possible. That's all. Sometimes we are quite good at it and sometimes we are not. That is how life is. Are you going to choose not trying to engage a *Lived Life* just because you might not always be good at it? Do you always succeed at what you attempt? Don't treat the notion of a *Lived Life* as an all or nothing thing. Instead, approach it as an ever evolving process that is propelled by your continuous effort to live the best life you can live.

A *Lived Life* should make you joyful. A Lived Life should contribute to the joy of others. If it doesn't, then what is the point? Samantabahdra's challenge to us, to bring joy to one person in the morning and to one person is the afternoon IS the challenge of a *Lived Life*. And again, sometimes we can and sometimes we can't. The important thing is to try.

Joy! Try it as a mantra throughout the day. Try saying to yourself from time to time during the day, "I am an inexhaustible source of joy." I'd be willing to bet that if you did this you find yourself smiling sometimes. When you do it will affect others. Try it and see what happens.

Joy in action is a special teaching for us in this century. Here is what Professor Wu Yangshen of the Shaanxi Normal University of China and Director of the Institute of Buddhist Studies there says:

> Of the greatest value in the 21st century is a positive attitude of Zen Joy.
>
> Our lives will be determined by our state of mind.
>
> A state of joy can turn iron into gold and bring sunshine to our lives.
>
> Once possessed of a state of Zen Joy each place in life is a good place, every even a good one and every person a good person.
>
> In a state of Zen Joy we can calmly emerge from darkness, escape from despair and climb our of the dry wells of life.

So far we have learned from Samatabahdra that there are certain actions we must take in our daily living if we want our lives to be lived fully. However, there is another kind of conduct or that Samatabahdra also models for us: Spiritual Conduct.

Before we stray too far off the path here, please keep in mind that there should be no difference between your daily conduct and your spiritual conduct. They should be one and the same. We are only separating them here for purposes of our discussion. To live our lives as best we can we must see all of our conduct as spiritual conduct.

Samantabahdra teaches us that, at its core, a *Lived Life* is a spiritual one where we embed our beliefs in our attitude and actions. Just as you and I are doing, he wanted to know what an active spiritual practice is. He wanted to know what such a practice required of him. He went so far as to ask the Buddha directly;

> *Greatly Compassionate World-Honored One, I would like to ask for all the bodhisattvas at this assembly, and for sentient beings of the degenerate age who are practicing Mahayana: let them hear this teaching of the realm of perfect enlightenment. How should we practice?*

A very simple question. In fact, he already possessed the answer. It was one of his names: Universal Good. Like him, we must act with goodness to all. I suppose this doesn't really explain to us 'how' does it? Here is an example of the beauty of Buddhism. It never leaves us with the nagging question of how, not even on the question of how to engage spiritual conduct.

Samatabahdra teaches us the very things the Buddha taught him about how to engage spiritual conduct. He teaches it to us in Book 21 of the <u>Avatamsaka Sutra</u> entitled *The Ten Practices*.

At this point in our exploration of what it means to engage a *Lived Life*, the first two of the ten practices are important: Joy and Beneficial Practices. The other eight are important, but for now let's just focus on the first two. The two go hand-in-hand. Let's try thinking of them as one rather than two. By that I mean, joy comes from the beneficial practices and the beneficial practices are the 'hows' of joy. The 'hows' of spiritual practice are these five taught by the Buddha to Samantabahdra:

1. divorce yourself from all bad acts
2. get rid of the idea of self
3. enter all the Buddha's teachings and explain them to others
4. abide in equanimity
5. be impartial towards all beings

If you stop and think about these five you can see that the benefits that flow from these practices flow both towards the other person and back to you.

If we divorce ourselves from bad acts we are not accumulating any karmnic residue. We don't suffer from remorse, shame, or guilt. We avoid all potential of doing harm to another.

If we can shed all notions of self, the I, me, mine, of our life we are left only with the thought of the other.

There is no more compassionate thing we can do than share the Buddha's teachings. Why do I say this is the most compassionate thing we can do? Because the teachings ARE the way our of suffering. They ARE the way to liberation. But, before we offer them to others we must, as Samantabadhra says, enter into them ourselves. This means we must understand them and live them ourselves first.

Equanimity, or the state of composure, can be a hard one to understand let alone practice. Equanimity is:

A state of psychological stability and composure which is undisturbed by experience of or exposure to emotions, pain, or other phenomena that may cause others to lose the balance of their mind.

One way to think of equanimity is to keep calm and balanced no matter what. Or, another way is to think of what happens when we are not in this state of mind. When we are not we are focused on ME and I am hogging all the space and sucking the air out of the room. When there is so much ME there is no room for WE.

Lastly, he says we must be impartial. Be careful here! This doesn't mean ambivalence. Impartiality means accepting the other person as they are and how they are in this moment. It also means never forgetting that the other person is a Buddha.

Samantabadhra is the flavor enhancer of our recipe for a *Lived Life*. We have learned that he spices our life with good intentions and conduct. A simple ingredient, but when added to our recipe the result is a complexity or aromas and tastes.

Before we leave Samantabahdra I'd like to share a little of his iconography with you. It might help you to recall his teachings and to keep a picture of him in your mind.

Samantabahdhra is most often depicted riding a three headed, six tusked, six legged white elephant. The six tusks represent the six senses and the six legs the six sense objects which give rise to the self. You may remember from one of our previous talks that all of experiences come from these six and from nowhere else. The three heads represent delusion, greed, and anger. Samantabadhra rides the elephant (the self/mind) to tame it and relieve it of its burdens. If we keep this image in mind it might help us as we face the challenges of riding our own white elephant.

Where are we in figuring out what a *Live Life* is? So far we have come to learn from the Bodhisattva teachers that a lived life asks us to listen compassionately, look with understanding and wisdom, and conduct ourselves with joy. That's not a bad way to live!

Let's end today with a story.

There was a philosopher who lived with several friends in a room only a few feet square. He was always happy and someone asked him: "with so many people squeezed together, what have you to be happy about?" He replied, "Living with friends I can exchange ideas and enjoy a good relationship with them , of course I'm happy."

In the course of time, all his friends got married and moved out leaving him living by himself, but he was as happy as ever. Again, someone asked him, "Living by yourself, what's there to be happy about?"

The philosopher replied, "I have a lot of books, each one is a friend and teacher, how can I not be happy in their company?"

Several years later the philosopher married and had a family and was given the ground floor on which to live. He was as cheerful as ever. He was asked, "the ground floor is so noisy how can you be so happy here?" He replied, "living here on the ground floor is really good. The moment I go in I'm with my family and it's convenient for going in and out and for going for walks. On the ground floor I can grow grass and flowers on any spare ground.

The lesson of this story is about attitude. If we have a joyful attitude and act on it, we can be like the philosopher and be happy anywhere. When we live life THIS WAY, we are becoming free, easy, and liberated. This is Joy in Action. This is living like Samantabadhra!

Reflection:

Use the following questions as subjects for meditation or journaling.

1. Have I ever considered myself a source of joy?
2. Where do I find joy in my life?
3. How often am I aware and mindful of the impact my itnetions, words, actions, even looks have on others?
4. How often do I smile and laugh?
5. What are the obstacles to my own experience of joy?
6. What keeps me from being a source of joy for others?
7. The most joyful person I know is _____. I say this because _____.

The Power Of Commitments

Let's begin with a story:

> Long ago, during the life of the Buddha known as Flower of Meditation and Enlightenment there was a young girl who became deeply concerned about her mother. Her mother had been disparaging the Three Jewels---The Buddha, The Dharma, and The Sangha. When her mother died the young girl became distraught. She was certain that her mother was going to the hell realm because she had spoken ill of the Three Jewels. The young girl sold whatever she could and made offerings to the Buddha so that the merit such offerings would generate could be transferred to her mother and thus she might be released from hell. After she made her offering she still was deeply troubled. She thought that if only she could know for sure if her

mother had, in fact, been re-born in the hell realm and if her offerings had released her. She went home and prayed to the Buddha Flower of Meditation and Enlightenment. This Buddha through the power of his commitments, transported her to the hell realm to show the young girl that, because of her offerings, her mother had been released from the hell realm. While the young girl was relieved that her mother had been spared from the hell realm, she was so touched by the vast number of those who still remained in the hell realm that she made this vow: I shall do my very best to relieve beings of their suffering forever in my future lives until all are saved from suffering and the hell realm.

Later, this young girl was re-born as thee Bodhisattva Ti Sang P'usa, or in the Sanskit, Khashitigabha, the Bodhisttva of the Great Vow to Help deliver All Beings.

For many of you this may sound like a rather fantastic story. After all, we Buddhist don't subscribe to prayers of intercession or the ability to be transported to another realm. But don't let the mythology interfere with the lesson being taught. We don't believe in fairy tales either, yet we tell them to our children. We tell the story of Khshitgarbha for exactly the same reason---this story, just like fairy tales, delivers a powerful message. The message of this story is that our commitments can have significant and far reaching effects. Khashitigarbha is the last of the four Bodhisattvas we look to as models for a *Lived Life*. He models for use just how powerful our commitments can be. He also teaches us that our intentions are the fuel that keeps our commitments lit.

Khshitgarbha is especially important in Chinese Buddhism. He Is almost universally present in all Chinese temples along with the Buddha and Kuan Yin. It is rare to find a Chinese temple that does not have an altar with all three. We are no exception. The altar to your left displays Khishitigarbha and Avaloketishavara (the male aspect of compassion). The altar to your right is a separate altar to Kuan Yin. Of course, in the middle is Buddha. The point I'm trying to make here is that Khashitigarbha holds special significance in the Chinese tradition that needs to be underscored. His vow of perseverance is deeply embedded in the Chinese consciousness and should be in ours as well.

While Compassion and Wisdom are the bookends of our way of a lived life and Samatabhadra flavors our life with joy, Khashitigarbha is the Bodhisattva who represents that one thing that must surround all the others. And, even though I say "he", let us not forget that in his past lives he was that young girl who first uttered the vow.

The recitation we do with regard to Khashitigarbha describes in clear terms that which must pervade everything we do is perseverance. The recitation doesn't just say "persevere", it gives a very specific method on how to persevere. As we listen to the words of the recitation listen for three commitments he stresses and the one, single method we must use:

> *I aspire to learn your way of being present when there is darkness, suffering, oppression and despair so that I can bring light, hope, relief, and liberation to those places. I am determined not to forget about or abandon those in desperate situations. I will do my best to establish contact with those who cannot find their way out of suffering, those who cries for help, justice, equality, and human rights are not being heard. I know that hell can be found in many places on earth. I will do my best not to create more hells on earth and to help transform the hells that already exist. I will practice in order to realize the qualities of perseverance so that, like the earth, I can always be supportive and faithful to those I need.*

Did you hear the three commitments: to bring hope, relief, and establish contact with those in need, to always be supportive to those in need. The method is — be present. Both the commitments and the method are straightforward enough, yet there is one word that is the essence of Khashitigarbha's vow, one word that gives it its unique texture --- *perseverance*. It is perseverance in all aspects of our *Lived Life* that we must learn from him. We must be like the young girl in our story who persevered in not just liberating her mother from the hell realm, but has lived many, many lives in fulfillment of her vow to liberate all beings from their hells.

Perseverance is the persistent pursuit of something even in the face of obstacles and difficulty. For those of your who remember the tsunami that hit Japan several years ago, or the massive earthquakes that hit China not long after the tsunami, you may recall the way the people affected by it reacted. They took care of each other. They didn't complain or act like victims.

They persisted in helping each other to recover. They persevered over the years and today the area is almost recovered even though it has been many years since the tragedy. I wonder how many of us could do what they did. What they did, and what we often find so difficult, is to persevere in the face of extraordinary difficulty. Perseverance and persistence is so engrained in their culture and it isn't in ours. Yes, we hear about it, but it is not a default place for us. We are too focused on quick, immediate results. Somewhere along the line we have lost our sense of the importance of perseverance and persistence. However, if you want to engage a *Lived Life* you must persevere and persist in engaging all the things we have talked about over the past few months.

What this bodhisattva teaches us is that we must persevere with our compassion, wisdom, conduct, and joy. No matter what challenges or obstacles we may face, if we are to live our lives fully and authentically we must always persevere in listening attentively, wholeheartedly, without hesitation or judgment to what is being said and what is not being said. We must persevere in being still so that we can look deeply into the heart of people and things so as to see the roots of suffering. We must persevere in being aware that every word, every look, every action, every smile can bring happiness to others. Can you see how Khashitigarbha's vow to persevere must be your vow as well? If we can't persevere in these practices we will never engage a *Lived Life*. When we gather these bodhisattvas together we have the opportunity to see not just what it takes to engage a *Lived Life*, but we can see that a *Lived Life* brings peace, ease, comfort, and joy.

In <u>The Way of the Bodhisattva</u>, Shantideva devotes a chapter to perseverance which he calls diligence. There is one verse in this chapter that strikes at the heart of the impact of perseverance. He says, *"for in such diligence enlightenment is found"*. Remember, we are using "liberation" instead of enlightenment. This simple statement is packed with implications. What he is saying is that through perseverance in engaging all the lessons we have learned from the bodhisattvas we will gain liberation not just for ourselves but for the benefit of all. That's some pretty powerful stuff!

We have talked about how these bodhisattvas are depicted. We noted Manjushri's sword that cuts through delusions and afflictions. We understand the imagery of Samantabadhra riding the three headed, six tusked, six legged elephant. Let's turn now to how Khashitigarbha is depicted.

Khashitigarbha has three aspects to the way he is depicted each of which can serve as a reminder to us of our vow of perseverance. As I mention each one take a moment to examine his statue on the altar to your left.

In his left hand he holds a staff with rings on the top. This is a monk's staff used in walking. The rings at the top make noise to scare off animals and insects so that they are not trampled on by the monk. I think we take the staff and give it a modern adaptation. As we walk through life we need the support of our convictions. Let's think of the staff as an embodiment of our vows. The rings at the top make noise to announce that we are coming to help relive suffering and bring joy. If we were to attach a fourth ring to the staff then we could say that each ring represents the attributes of the four bodhisattvas: listening, looking, acting, persevering.

Khashitigarbha is also shown holding what looks like a globe or ball in his right hand. This globe or ball is a Mani Jewel. The Mani Jewel is thought to possess wish fulfilling powers beyond description. He carries it not to fulfill his own wishes, but to make its power available to fulfill the wishes of all sentient beings. It is brought to them to fulfill their wishes for an end to suffering, a ceasing of the endless cycle of samsara, and a life of happiness and joy. It should remind us that we too carry with us a Mani Jewel---the power of the Buddha's teachings and the power of our own intentions and commitments.

Lastly, he is shown wearing a five leafed crown. In each leaf is a meditating Buddha. This is to remind us that the power and energy of our vows, thoughts, words, actions, and even smiles arises from our perseverance toward meditative concentration in all that we do.

We are now familiar with the four bodhisattvas who model for us the core principles of a *Lived Life*: compassion, wisdom, action, joy, and perseverance. Remember, engaging these principles in our life means we must look, listen, speak, and act with utmost attention and wholeheartedness. No matter what life may throw at us we must persist in bringing the lessons of the bodhisattvas into fullness in our lives. If can, we are not just living our lives, but we are living them with happiness and joy. Isn't that the ultimate wish we can grant for everyone?

Reflection:

Use each of the following sentences from the Khshitigarbha recitation as an object for meditation or for journaling.

1. I aspire to be present where there is darkness, suffering, oppression and despair.
2. I aspire to being light, hope, relief, and liberation to the darkness.
3. I will not forget or abandon those in desperate situations.
4. I will do my best not create more hells on earth.
5. I will practice perseverance and persistence so that I can always be supportive and faithful to those in need.

The Eight Winds of Discontent

I have a bit of a tangent I would like us to take today as we continue our journey towards a *Lived Life*.

Over the past few months we have moved from an examination of our fears, including the fear of a *Lived Life*, to the examination of a list of attributes and practices taught by the bodhisattvas to help us engage a *Lived Life* of Joy. Today, I'd like us to stop and consider what gets in our way. What are the things that keep us distracted? What things do we gravitate towards that shackle us to our fears and habits? In our Buddhist practice we call these obstacles the Eight Worldly Concerns, or the Eight Winds of Discontent. As part of our practice we should take inventory every once in awhile to see how these Eight Winds are affecting us. Today is just a good a day as any to stop and take that inventory. Consider this an introduction to the hidden obstacles to a *Lived Life*. The image of wind is a good one. The air around us is sometimes still, sometimes a gentle breeze, at other times it is wild and raging just as our thoughts and emotions can.

The Eight Winds we will take stock of today are set out in "The Book of Eights" in the Anguttara Nikaya. In this chapter the Buddha teaches us how these Eight Winds can blow us off the perfect center of our lives and keep us from engaging a *Lived Life*. He teaches us:

> *An uninstructed worldling meets gain and loss, disrepute and fame, blame and praise, and pleasure and pain and does not reflect thus: that these are impermanent, suffering, and subject to change. Instead, gain obsesses his mind and loss obsesses his mind. Fame obsesses her mind and disrepute obsesses her mind. Blame obsesses his mind and praise obsesses his mind. Pleasure obsesses her and pain obsesses her mind. She is attracted to gain and repelled by loss. He is attracted to*

fame and repelled by disrepute. She is attracted to praise and repelled by blame. He is attracted to pleasure and repelled by pain. This involved with attraction and repulsion they are not freed from birth, from old age and death, from sorrow, lamentation, pain, dejection and anguish. They are not freed from suffering.

Notice that there are actually four pairs of opposing winds rather than eight individual ones. Notice also that each of the pairs is one of extremes. As the Buddha reiterates over and over, we must find the middle way between extremes, including these four pair of extremes.

Before we take a closer look at each pair, let's try to understand how the brain works in relation to these winds. To do this we must turn to science. Buddhism has a healthy respect for science. We hold no animosity towards it. We embrace it. We embrace it because, time and time again, science has demonstrated the truth of the Buddha's teachings. What I am about to share with you next from the world of science may take some real effort on your part to understand. As with much of science, it is written for the fellow scientist and not the layperson, so we may have to struggle a bit to understand what the scientists are saying. With respect to our habits, such as those identified in the Eight Winds, researchers have observed that:

> *The brain arbitrates between the habit and goal-directed valuation systems by assigning control to the system that at any given time has the less uncertain estimate of the true value of the actions. As the quality of the estimates that are made by the habit system increases with experience, this means in practice that the habit system should gradually take over from the goal-directed system.*

> *Second, in most circumstances the quality of decision making depends on the brain's ability to assign control to the valuation system that makes the best value forecasts.*

Think about this for a moment. What these researches have learned is that the brain will always default to our habitual way of thinking and to those habits that our experience tells us makes the best forecast of our future. What they also point out is that we come to trust these habits without ever calling them into question. If we are to break free from these habits, if we are to be on guard against the habitual winds that buffet us, we must come to understand where our habits lie. We must identify what new habits we want to replace them with if they are not leading us to the truth, freedom, acceptance, love, compassion, and the joy of a *Lived Life*. This is what the Eight Winds of Discontent help us to do --- to identify the habits that inhibit our ability to engage a *Lived Life*.

The Eight Winds are the winds of our habits. These habits are the real obstacles to a *Lived Life*. Our habits are comfortable, predictable, even if they are harmful. That is why we have such a difficult time breaking them. They are just too damned easy to ride.

As we sit here today, ready to engage our *Lived Lives,* we must take the time to examine the very things that can inhibit our lives. These Eight Winds are the very things that have, and always will, get in our way.

Gain and Loss.

Of the four pairs, this wind of gain and loss is the one is that drives us to acquire material things, friendships, relationships, or anything that we could end up calling "mine". The opposing wind is the wind of fear of losing what one already has, the loss of what is "mine".

There have been a lot of studies about which if these two winds is the more effective motivator of behavior. In fact, the amount of research and the number of theories is vast. Yet, one thing that all the researchers agree on is that both are very, very strong motivators. However, as between the two, loss is the stronger motivator. This means that it is the wind of loss that blows stronger and more relentlessly than the wind of gain. Why is this?

The research says it's because losing what we already have is more stressful than failing to gain what we want. The psychological impact of losing is thought to be twice as powerful as the pleasure of gaining. What is even more important to realize is, we often make our quickest and most irrational decisions based on our fear of loss. Fear of losing what is mine is a powerful wind that blows through our lives. It has the strength of a hurricane or tornado.

You might be thinking, "okay, I get that, but what about the wind of gain? How strong is that wind?" You may even be disagreeing with what the research shows because you believe your experiences about wanting something and not getting it have been tougher for you to handle. That is because you have not thought about this before. When you take the time to think about these opposing winds, really think about them, you will discover that the research is right.

The best way to get a feel for the power of the wind of gain is to observe how often we speak the phrase "I need". To need something is to say that your very life depends on it. It includes things like food, water, shelter, safety. If you listen carefully, not just to yourself, but to others, you will hear that expression "I need" over and over again. The truth is, what you or the other person is saying is that you "want". Most have us have our needs satisfied. Our wants are a whole different dimension. The wind of gain is the wind that carries the voice that says, 'I want." If we are aware of just how often we use the phrases "I need" or "I want", we can get a sense of the power of this wind. What we can observe is the persistent and relentless howling of the wind of gain. Of all the winds, this pair, the winds of gain and loss may be, at least for some of us, the winds that cause us the most damage. These are the winds that keep blowing us off the course of a *Lived Life*.

Fame and Disrepute

No one wants to be thought about negatively so most of us seek to develop a good reputation. That is our nature. None of us wants a bad reputation. What the Buddha is describing in this pair of winds is the drive we have to be seen as something other than who we are; to be famous or idolized even in a small way. It is the obsession to be seen as above, apart, or better than others.

I suppose one could argue that the pursuit of fame is an expression of discontent with who you are. At its core, this pursuit of a good reputation is the great separator---by seeking fame we push others down and away so that we can be seen by as better than, or at least it is the delusion we create about ourselves. What we often forget is that the pursuit of fame leads to others thinking less of us, not more. This is the easiest of winds to experience. It isn't as rough and wild as the winds of gain or loss. This is a soothing wind. It is also a deceitful wind.

The wind of disrepute, or a negative reputation, is like the fear of loss. It is the fear of being seen as below as opposed to above others. It is the fear of separation----the very thing that the desire for fame creates.

Here is something interesting to consider with regard to fame and disrepute. The word fame and reputation mentioned often in the sutras. For example, in the chapter entitled "The Wise" in the <u>Dhammapada</u> there is the repeated mention of how to gain a good reputation. Is that inconsistent with what we have just learned about these two winds? Why would the Buddha talk about having a good reputation? I think what the Buddha is saying is not to pursue the reputation for its own sake which is what the wind does. Rather, he is saying that doing good for its own sake leads others to "hold one dear", but, seeking reputation for reputations sake is harmful. Just do good and that is enough. Seek nothing for your actions. That is enough. It is perfect. If others think well of you, okay. Don't seek their opinion of you. Do you understand?

In the end neither a good or bad reputation last. Both are temporary, fleeting, and subject to change. We must never forget this.

I'd like to share a short Zen story that highlights the teaching on the winds of fame and disrepute.

> *Kai-Chu, the great Zen teacher of the Meiji era, was the head of Tofuki, a cathedral in Kyoto. One day the governor of Kyoto called upon him for the first time. His attendant presented the governor's calling card which read: Kitagaki, Governor of Kyoto.*
>
> *"I have no business with such a fellow" said Kai-Chu, "tell him to get out of here."*
>
> *The attendant carried the card back with apologies.*
>
> *"This was my error" said the governor and with a pencil he scratched out the words Governor of Kyoto. He returned the card to the master's attendant saying, "ask your*

teacher again."

The attendant returned the altered card to the Zen teacher who said, " Oh, it is Kitagaki, I want to see that fellow".

Blame and Praise

Think of each of these as having two aspects: each has one aspect to it that is internal and one that is external. The internal places blame or praise on ourselves while the external places it on others. I like to think of these two not so much as winds as breezes, especially the internal aspects. Think of them as the kind of breeze that just doesn't let up. Sometimes they can build to a howling wind, but when they subside they still continue to blow just enough to be felt, just like the breeze you feel along the ocean. It's always there and you can smell its saltiness.

As for the internal breeze, we should neither blame nor praise ourselves. This can be challenging. You might say that self-blame can be a good thing because it helps remind us of where we have caused harm and need to atone. We could also argue that self-praise is a reminder to repeat good things we have done. Perhaps, but when we obsess about either one we get all tied up in knots and our ability to be present and mindful is cut-off. When we are cut-off we are never present, we cannot engage the things the bodhisattvas teach us, and we are very, very far removed from a *Lived Life*.

There is an interesting psychological effect called the "negativity effect" which says that we are, by nature, quicker to place blame on negative attitudes and actions that we are to give praise for a positive attitude or action. In other words, we a prone to negative reactions and blaming and there is not an equally corresponding inclination to offer praise.

If we take the "negativity effect" and use it as a mirror on ourselves what might we learn? What happens when we see that we are prone to view even our own attitudes and actions from a perspective of blame? Does that help us understand them or change them? What happens if we become mindful of this in ourselves? Is it possible that our mindfulness is enough to facilitate some change that will bring us closer to the truth, freedom, love and the *Lived Life* we've been talking about?

Then there is the external aspect --- our inclination towards blaming others. Here the negativity effect is even bolder and the wind blows harder. When we rush to judge others, when we rush to speak ill of them, what are we really doing? Who are we to judge in the first place? Who are we to assign any blame to anyone? Each of knows the answers to these questions, yet when the wind starts to rise it always seems to blow those answers away leaving us right back in the middle of our old habits.

As for praise, if the researchers are correct, then this is something we are much less inclined to offer others. Why do you think that is? It's a very interesting question to ponder. And here is the real challenge with praise: can we offer it without any expectation? Or, are we offering praise so that the other will think more highly of us which, in turn, leads us right back to seeking fame versus a bad reputation. Very tricky thing is praise. The moment you offer it with any expectation on the part of the other person you aren't offering praise; you are being selfish.

Pleasure and Pain

This is perhaps the easiest of the four pairs of winds. At least that is how it might appear at first glance, but what separates these winds from the others and makes them more of a challenge is that our obsession with the pursuit of pleasure and the avoidance of pain tends to add to the velocity of these winds. These winds are strong enough without our help, but we are all too eager to make them blow louder and longer than the other winds.

If we find ourselves riding the wind of pleasure and can catch ourselves, we can see that obsession for pleasure leads to addictive behaviors, the utmost indulgence of the ego and the exploitation of other people, resources, energy, you name it. I suppose we could say it is the mother/father of greed. The Buddha teaches us that there is maybe nothing that so interferes with our mindfulness, our full presence in the moment, our ability to be loving, kind, and compassionate, than the obsession for pleasure. Remember that the pleasure the Buddha is talking about is all sense pleasure: eye, ear, nose, tongue, body, mind. Be careful though. There is no prohibition against experiencing sense pleasure. The prohibition is against the obsessive and relentless pursuit of it.

The opposing wind is the wind that blows us into the avoidance of pain. Again, at first glance, one could say that this is a good thing. After all, isn't our practice all about the cessation of suffering and stress. Yes, but to obsess about avoiding pain takes us away from life. It keeps us from accepting and being in what we have at this moment. Sometimes that is what our lives present and to act so as to hide from the pain of living keeps us from living our lives as it presents itself, from moment to moment. Pain and suffering is life. It is the first Noble Truth taught by the Buddha: Life is Suffering. There is another aspect to this truth. No matter how hard the wind of avoidance of pain may blow, it never, ever blows it all away.

As we engage our lives in the many ways we have examined over the past several months we must be ever mindful that there are eight strong winds that can blow us off the perfect place of our lives. If we pursue these winds, obsess about them, and want to ride them we are not engaging our life---we are engaging our ego, the source of all the stress and suffering we experience.

Reflection:

The following statements should be the subject of a meditation. It takes the stillness of meditation to probe these questions wholeheartedly.

1. Do I find myself at times pursuing things just for the pleasure of them?
2. Do I obsess over losing things that I already have?
3. Am I sometimes focused on saying or doing things so that people with hold me in high regard?
4. Am I ever anxious that people will think poorly of me?
5. Am I quick to place blame on others?
6. Is my first response often that I am the one to blame?
7. How easy is it for me to offer praise to others?
8. Do I without praise for others and if so, why?
9. Do I sometimes find myself seeking pleasure for pleasure's sake?
10. What is my typical response to the threat of pain and pain itself?

A Mind of No Anticipation

Listen to these words from Master Hung Ying-ming's, <u>The Master of the Three Ways</u>:

> *When your thoughts are at peace and have become transparent, you see the true form of the mind.*
>
> *When your feelings are at rest and have become tranquil, you understand the true movements of the mind.*
>
> *When your disposition is disinterested and totally calm, you obtain the true flavor of the mind.*
>
> *There is nothing that can rival these three..*
>
> *Only in the peace obtained in the midst of activity is found the true sphere of one's original nature.*

I offer these words from the Master as we lurch (and I use that term deliberately) into the holiday season. He offers us some wonderful advice to help us through this often trying time of year. This time of year, this Christmas/New Year Season is also a both a challenge to and an opportunity for our engaging a *Lived Life.*

This is one of the most active times of year and keeping our peace and calm can be tough at times. But, he says, if we can keep our thoughts transparent, our feelings at rest, and our disposition calm in the middle of all this activity, then we can have a peaceful and calm holiday. What he is describing is a *Lived Holiday Season!*

What he suggests, I think, is that we develop what I like to call, "The Mind of No Anticipation". It is in anticipating things that our mind becomes aroused and agitated. It is in anticipation that our minds make up all sorts of story telling most of which is pure fiction. And, when our minds are aroused in this way we find ourselves living something the Buddha taught, but not in a good way: we become what we think---we become our own agitation. So let's spend a few minutes this morning reflecting on what a Mind of No Anticipation might be like. As we do, ask yourself this: is the Mind of No Anticipation the mind of a *Lived Life?*

Let's begin by considering a few statistics. Recent studies by the American Psychological Association suggest that a full 68% of people say they suffer abnormal stress during the holidays. The American Hospital Association studied seasonal heart attacks over a twelve year period and found that there were one third more heart attacks in December and January. Is there a corollary between the two? If someone is engaged in a *Lived Life* what are the chances they will be a statistic? Slim I'd guess.

The AHA researchers thought they would find that seasonal temperature might be a significant factor, but what they found is, that while it was a factor, emotional stress associated with the holidays and over indulgence were statistically more significant.

It seems then, that a lot of what happens to us during the holidays comes from not from external factors but of our own making. Everything comes from our choices. It is the anticipating mind that chooses while the non-anticipating mind is at ease and ready to accept what is, just as it is.

We know that our emotions are of our own choosing---they do not happened to us. They are not the fault of some other person or some outside factor. They have one, simple origin---our own mind. It is our mind that anticipates, assumes, that projects onto people and events our own thoughts and mostly they have little relationship to the truth. Looking back to on what we have learned so far, we can say that the anticipating mind likes to ride the Eight Winds of Discontent and the self the mind creates is very willing to ride along.

Let's take one example. One of the most often reported stressors during the holidays is a family gathering. Most of us look forward to them on the one hand, but are anxious on the other hand. We begin to play out what we anticipate will happen. We justify our story to ourselves arguing that we are right because such and such happened in the past or so and so did X in the past. We are caught in the wind of blame. The wind blows so strongly that we convince ourselves that the past is going to repeat itself. All too often we convince ourselves that this year it will be even worse. Before we know it, the wind is howling, our emotions are accelerating along with our heart rate and the nausea in our belly. The truth is, and by the truth I mean that which we really know, is that we have no idea what the gathering will be like. When we allow ourselves to be blown into anticipating we are no longer just thinking about what is coming, we become active participants in causing it to unfold just as we think it will. Remember, we become what we think. That too is a truth.

The question then is: HOW do we change from an anticipating mind to a non-anticipating mind? The first step is what we discussed about the Eight Winds and our old habits: be mindful and aware of the effects they are having on you.

Even more than that, we must maintain our awareness and mindfulness in all things. Many of you have heard me say this before, there is a difference between awareness and mindfulness. We need to remind ourselves of the difference because knowing this difference is the first step in the HOW to change to a non-anticipating mind.

Awareness is a recognition of what is happening. For now, we want to focus on the awareness of our thoughts. We want to keep our focus very, very sharp so that we can acknowledge our holiday thoughts. We must be careful not to analyze them or evaluate them; just acknowledge that we are having them. Acknowledgement means something more than observing them as they pass. IF we want to be really aware of our thoughts then we must see them fully in all their details. This means we must engage them on some level. We must be able to "witness" them. A witness sees with clarity. A witness can recall details. A witness observes closely and remains apart from the thought yet can identify every aspect of it. That is what we mean by awareness of our thoughts. This is where we begin, with a clear, unobstructed view of the thoughts. For example, maybe you have a thought of your mother or brother or sister coming for the holidays. Your thought leaves an emotional mark. Maybe you can hear their voice, its tone, its attitude. You can see them as if they are there with you. You are responding in some physical way. Perhaps your stomach is churning, your shoulders are getting tight, your jaw clenches. Then you become aware of the emotions rising. This is what we mean by awareness. This is HOW you begin to shift your mind.

Mindfulness is your reaction to your thought. It is important to be able to separate the physical and emotional response contained in the thought from the physical and emotional response to it. One way to move from awareness to mindfulness is to recognize the point at which you shift from witnessing the thought and all it contains, to evaluating and analyzing it. When we engage the thought in this way we are now reacting to it. We must be mindful of out reaction to the very thought we are witnessing. This requires a different level of insight. Here, we are not witnessing the thought, which for all intents and purposes is already a past event, but we are witnessing our present reaction to it. Do you understand the difference?

Awareness is the witnessing of the thought in all of its details. Awareness is the bridge from the past, the thought, to the present, mindful reaction to it. Once you understand this difference you know HOW to move the mind from anticipation to non-anticipation. The anticipating mind remains stuck. In fact, we remain so stuck that we take our awareness of the thought to be the reality of the thing itself and we believe that it is our present reality. The mind is so clever that we believe this thing we imagine and assume to be true not just now, but is an absolutely accurate prediction of the future. This is complete nonsense because we cannot know the future at all.

We become what we believe. Do you want to become what you anticipate? Or, do you want the peace and calm that comes with non-anticipation? When you move to non-anticipation then you are truly free to experience whatever it is that will happen and you are liberated from the stress and anxiety of your anticipations. There is also one more thing. When you move to a non-anticipating mind you give the gift of freedom to those people and events you have been stressed about. Think for a moment about how this might make your holidays different.

Reflection:

Take some time to reflect on a song written in the 19th century by the Tibetan yogi Shabkar. This is a song about what the mind is like when it is free of anticipation and abides in its pure, natural state:

> *When one looks towards one's own mind---The root of all phenomenon---There is nothing but vivid emptiness. Nothing there concrete to be taken as real.*
>
> *It is present as transparent, utter openness, without outside, without inside---An all-pervasiveness without boundary and without direction.*
>
> *The wide-open expanse of the view, the true condition of the mind, is like the sky, like space, without center, without edge, without aim.*
>
> *By leaving whatever I experience relaxed in ease, just as it is, I have arrived at the vast plain that is the absolute expanse.*
>
> *In the absolute expanse of awareness all things are blended into that single taste, but relatively, each and every phenomenon is distinctly, clearly seen. Wondrous!*

Without entering into the narrow rock gorge which is mind watching for stillness and movement, without being caught in the snare of "views" created by the intellect, without flying into the dark clouds of dull states of mind, without plunging into the storm of agitated thinking, the great bird, my own mind, flew freely into the wide open sky of the absolute expanse.

Eyes completely open, encompassing a hundred horizons, utterly at ease, the bird of mind wings its way---What a Delight!

Even more than the sky is the view, emptiness; there the sun of love and the moon of compassion arose and again and again I made boundless prayers to benefit the teachings and all beings. May all disease and epidemics of disease, all famine, and all wars be ended and may all have happiness and joy.

A Lived Life

Here we are at the end of our practice period and the end of our exploration of what it means to engage a *Lived Life*. If it hasn't dawned on you yet, a *Lived Life* is the life of the bodhisattva; one who aspires not just for their own enlightenment, but the enlightenment of everyone. With enlightenment comes liberation. With liberation comes joy. With joy comes compassion, kindness, equanimity, and bliss. This what the Buddha teaches us and this is what is so urgently needed in the world today. Those of you who have come along on this exploration know this well. I have no doubt that each of you will strive to do your best to engage a *Lived Life, the life of a bodhisattva*.

So, how should we end? We could restate everything we've talked about, but why rehash what we already know. Let's end with something different.

Each and every one of us is a farmer. We are like corn farmers---we plant a single crop. Like the corn farmer, we prepare our fields, plant one type of seed, provide it with nutrients, make sure it gets watered, and, eventually, we harvest the crop. We plant row after row of single seeds just as the corn farmer does. Just as each kernel of corn produces a stalk of corn and each stalk of corn produces 2 or 3 ears of corn and each of ear of corn produces hundreds of kernels, each of which is a seed with the potential for another stalk, 2-3 more ears, and hundreds more kernels. The seeds we plant are just like this. From a single see rises the potential for hundreds, if not thousands, of additional seeds. The seed I'm talking about today is the seed of karma. We cannot end our exploration of a *Lived Life* without returning to karma.

We often think of karma as a single act with a single result, but that is nor true. Every intention, word, or action is like the single seed of corn. One single seed of karma can produce one, two, three, even hundreds of results and each result can be a seed for further karmic action. If you understand nothing more about Buddhism, understand your nature as a corn farmer. Understand that every intention, word, and action you take, not matter how small or larger is just like a kernel of corn---packed with the potential for many, many results. Each action we take can, like the single seed of corn, produce hundreds of consequences each of which carries the potential to become a new seed.

The Tibetan yogin Shabkar reminds us:

Whatever you have done, good or bad, in your past lives; whatever you do in this life will have an effect on future lifetimes. So, you must be aware of the consequences of your actions. . . .

In short, every action has its corresponding result. So the Buddha said, And the Buddha's words never deceive. Acknowledge their truth and exercise your discernment. This is crucial.

Over the past several months we have been exploring the impact our recollection of the four bodhisattvas can have on our commitment to engage a *Lived Life*. As we became acquainted with each of them, we learned how to discern those things we must do that result in wholesome karma from those that have negative karmic impacts. Each of the bodhisattvas we studied is an example of how to plant only wholesome kernels of karma from which many, many wholesome results are possible. Think of them as organic kernels of karma, not some kind of genetically modified version. They are the purest forms of karmic seeds. They are the embodiment of virtuous conduct that has only positive karmic results. Each one of them, in their own way, models not just a specific wholesome action, but each also models the four-part process that results in karmic effect.

Every karmic action has four distinct parts to it:

the basis,

the intention,

the course of action, and

the completion of the action.

Let's take just one of the bodhisattvas as an example of how the karmic process works.

Kuan Yin/Avaloketishavara, the bodhisattva of Great Compassion, teach us that listening is the most fundamental act of compassion and that it can result in significant wholesome or positive karma. Using her as an example of the four part process we can learn:

1. the basis is others (and this is almost always the basis)
2. the intention---to listen wholeheartedly and attentively to the other
3. the course of action---listening
4. the completion of the action---listening until the other is completely finished and

> we have maintained our wholeheartedness and attentiveness.

On the surface these seems pretty easy doesn't it? Just sit and listen to the other until they are finished. If that's what you are thinking you have missed something very important. You are forgetting that this type of listening requires us to be attentive and wholehearted. You must maintain this kind of listening constantly just as Samantabadhra teaches us. That is what makes this so hard. It is also why it carries such potential for positive karma.

You might ask: what happens if I don't complete the process or don't' complete it perfectly. What then? There is still a karmic result, but the weight or quality of it is less or greater depending on the degree to which you have completed the steps. Don't get caught up in the ultimate outcome. That is your ego speaking. Just do your best and that in itself is perfect enough.

Let's take one more example, this time looking at a negative karmic effect. Let's take a look at lying.

1. the basis---another person who can hear the lie
2. the intention---the wish to deceive a specific person about a particular subject.
3. The course of action---verbal or something more subtle such as implying the lie through your physical conduct or failure to speak
4. Completion of the action---when the person hears and understands the lie.

We don't need to dwell on the impact this has. We all have enough experience with lying to know its consequences.

The karmic process is something that we must always appreciate as we move through our lives. Because, in the end, it is our karma that drives the course of our lives and the consequences we experience. Stop for a minute! Just imagine what life would be like if we persevered with compassion, wisdom and action all of which are directed by a persistent attitude towards joy? Can you even begin to imagine what a life like that would be like? Of course you can. It's the *Lived Life* we have been working towards since the beginning of this practice period.

Even though the bodhisattvas teach us how to engage a *Lived Life,* sometimes we need a different perspective. The result is the same, but the approach is a little different. Once again, Buddhism provides us with this different perspective. In fact, Buddhism provides us with some very specific guidelines to follow should we choose to do so. They are called, "The Ten Virtuous Deeds". They are the seeds of positive karma just as the "The Non-Virtuous Deeds" are the seeds of negative karma. These virtuous deeds flow from the actions the bodhisattvas have modeled for us. They are broken into three categories: three of the body, four of speech, and three of the mind. Regardless of the category, each virtuous deed listed is quite specific. Here are the "Ten Virtuous Deeds" by category:

Body:
1. protect life
2. be honest
3. maintain proper sexual conduct

Speech:
1. tell the truth
2. avoid gossip
3. avoid slander
4. speak gentle words that bring happiness to others

Mind:
1. rejoice in the good fortune of others
2. have only thoughts that are beneficial to others
3. have correct views.

Maybe we should all print this list and carry it around with us or post it on our refrigerators.

Ten rather simple intentions and actions each of which is a single see packed full of potential for thousands more seeds every one of which is wholesome. Plant these seeds and you are engaged in a *Lived Life*. If you, then a *Lived Life* is effortless.

Too often we think of karma as something only an individual can create. This is an incorrect view of karma. the Buddha teaches in the <u>Surangama Nikaya</u> that there is a second kind of karma, a shared karma. Just as each of us alone can create karma, two or more persons can create a shared karma. You could also call it accumulated karma or group karma. Maybe we should call it a karma conspiracy.

A karma conspiracy works like this. Take, for example, two different groups. The first group jointly takes action to discriminate against others, to limit their rights or actions. Another group takes action to provide opportunity and relieve the suffering of the same persons the other group has targeted. Each group speaks and acts together. In each case not only does each individual incur a personal karmic result for both their individual action, but also for the action taken by the group. We can take this one step further. Suppose each group then organizes with other small groups into a larger and larger group. As the group increases in number and size, the karmic results likewise increase. It doesn't take long before the karmic web of each person, sub-group, and larger group is intertwined. There are inconceivable billions of consequences to these actions.

This is something we must all understand about karma: it is this ever evolving and expanding web of action and consequence that is caused by every action we take individually and every action we take with others. This should have a profound impact on you. So profound that Master Hsuan Hua, in his <u>Commentary to the Surangama Sutra,</u> says that when we read the section of karma, "you should experience terror. You should be shocked".

We should be. When we understand that karma permeates everything then we must also know that our ability to shape our lives for wholesome karma requires a depth of personal commitment that can be challenging even under the best of circumstances. But this should no deter us at all. It should prompt us to do our best no matter what. We must be good corn farmers sowing only wholesome seeds.

Can you imagine what life would be like if we persevered and persisted in sowing only the seeds of compassion, wisdom, and action with an attitude towards joy? Can you imagine the impact this would have?!

As we close out our discussion on what it means to engage a *Lived Life*, let me suggest that we make one last commitment. Let us commit from this day forward to be farmers engaged in a *Lived Life*, sowing only virtuous seeds. Let's also commit to building a community or farmers to support and encourage each other.

We alone are the creators of a *Lived Life*. Each and every moment of our lives is an opportunity to create happiness and joy or stress and suffering. It is our choice alone. For those who came along these past few months on the journey towards a *Lived Life*, you know the choices to make and the consequences that can result from those choices. A consistent attitude towards joy combined with persistent, whole hearted attentiveness, compassionate listening, a still and quite looking into the heart of people and things, and actions rooted in kindness, leads to a life lived so that stress and suffering are alleviated. This is what you have chosen to do. The is both the challenge and the reward of a *Lived Life*.

Remember these words of the Buddha:

The ripening result of an action

Does not occur to the earth

To the water

To the wind, or

To the elements.

It only occurs to the one who created the cause.

The Final Reflection:

The following poem by Master Hongzhi entitled, "Guidepost for the Hall of Pure Bliss" (translated by Taigen Dan Leighton) is a guidepost to the Lived Life. I urge you to get a copy and make it part of your regular contemplative practice. There is much in it that will remind you of what we have learned these past few months.

By seeking appearance and sound one cannot truly find the Way.

The deep source of realization

Comes with constancy, bliss, self, and purity.

Its purity is constant, its bliss is myself.

The two are mutually dependent, like firewood and fire.

The self's bliss is not exhausted, constant purity has no end.

Deep existence is beyond forms,

Wisdom illuminates the inside of the circle.

Inside the circle the self vanishes,

Neither existence nor non existence.

Intimately conveying spiritual energy,

It subtly turns the mysterious pivot.

When the mysterious pivot finds opportunity to turn,

The original light auspiciously appears.

When the mind's conditioning has not yet sprouted,

How can words and images be distinguished?

Who is it that distinguishes them?

Clearly understand and know by yourself.

Whole and inclusive with inherent insight,

It is not concerned with discriminating thought.

When discriminating thought is not involved,

It's like white reed flowers shining in the snow.

One beam of light's gleam permeates the vastness.

The gleam permeates all directions,

From the outset not covered or concealed.

Catching the opportunity to emerge,

Amid transformations it flourishes.

Following appropriately amid transformations,

The pure bliss is unchanged.

Sky encompasses it, ocean seals it,

Every moment without deficiency.

In the achievement without deficiency,

Inside and outside are interfused.

All Dharmas transcend their limits, all gates are wide open.

Through the open gates are the byways of playful wandering.

Dropping off senses and sense objects is like

The flowers of our gazing and listening falling away.

Gazing and listening are only distant conditions

Of thousands of hands and eyes.

The others die from being too busy, but I maintain continuity.

In the wonder of continuity

Are no traces of subtle identifications.

With purity is bliss, with silence is illumination.

The house of silent illumination is the hall of pure bliss.

Dwelling in peace and forgetting hardship,

Let go of adornments and become genuine.

The motto of becoming genuine: nothing is gained by speaking.

The goodness of Vimalakirti enters the gate of non-duality.

Selected Bibliography

<u>Cultivating the Empty Field</u>. Taigen Dan Leighton. Tuttle Library of Enlightenment, North Clarendon, VT, 2000.

<u>Hsin Hsin Ming.</u> Richard B. Clark, *trans.* Amazon, Kindle Edition.

<u>Master of the Three Ways: Reflections of a Chinese Sage on Living a Satisfying Life</u>. Yung Ying-Ming: William Scott Wilson, *trans.*. Shambala Publications, Inc., Boston, MA, 2009.

<u>Practicing the Path: A Commentary on the Lamrim Chensmo.</u> Yangsi Rinpoche. Wisdom Publications, Boston, MA, 2003.

<u>The Anguttara Nikaya (The Numerical Discourses of the Buddha).</u> Bhikkhu Bodi, *trans.*. Wisdom Publications, Somerville, MA 2012.

<u>The Art of Living and Dying</u>. Osho. Watkins Publishing, London, UK, 2000, 2013.

<u>The Book of Secrets</u>. Osho. St Martin's Griffin, New York, NY 1974.

<u>The Dhammapada</u>. K. Sri Dhammananda, *trans.*. Sasana Abhiwurdhi Wardhana Society, Kuala Lampur, Malaysia, 1988.

<u>The Flower Ornament Scripture: A Translation of the Avatamsaka Sutra</u>. Thomas Cleary, *trans.*. Shambala Publications, Inc. Boston, MA, 1993.

The Life of Shabkar: The Autobiography of a Tibetan Yogin. Mathieu Ricard, Jacob Leschly, Eric Schmidt, Marilyn Silverstone, and Lodro Palmo *trans.*. State University of New York Press, New York, NY, 1994.

The Lotus Sutra. Burton Watson, *trans.*. Columbia University Press, New York, NY, 1993.

The Path of Love: On the Songs of Kabir. Osho. Osho Media International, New York, NY, 1976, 2013.

The Samyutta Nikaya. Bhikkhu Bodi, *trans.*. Wisdom Publications, Somerville, MA, 2000.

The Surangama Sutra. Venerable Master Hsuan Hua, commentator. Bhuddist Text Translation Society, Ukiah, CA, 2009.

The Twenty Seven Verses on Mind Training. Lama Je Tsongkapa. www.tenzinpeljo.de

The Way of the Bodhisattva. Padamkara Translation Group, *trans.*. Shambala Publications, Inc., Boston, MA, 1997, 2006.

Author

The Venerable Deok Wun is an ordained Bhikkhu in the Korean Zen tradition. He is the founding Abbot of the Grand rapids Buddhist Temple and Zen Center in Grand Rapids, Michigan. He started the temple in 1999 without a single member and limited services. Today the temple has an active membership of over 150 and a casual membership numbering several hundred. The temple now has another full time monk, a Soto Priest, a part time monk, and two Dharma Teachers.

The temple offers classes and workshops several times a week in additional to its regular services. The temple offers a Buddhist Based Addiction Recovery Program three times a week and a similarly based Alanon program once a week. The temple also offers a Dharma School for children during Sunday Service and it is staffed by a full time teacher.

The temple is located in downtown Grand Rapids.

For information check the temple website grzen.org or call 616 822 2465

Made in the USA
Monee, IL
18 August 2024